1/08

Precept Ministries
P.O. Box 182218
Chattanooga
Tennessee
37422

Thanks,
Beloved
Eccl. 4:9

Love,
Jack & Kay

D1413807

EMMAUS PUBLIC LIBRARY
11 EAST MAIN STREET
EMMAUS, PA 18049

The Peace & Power
of Knowing God's Name

THE PEACE & POWER of KNOWING GOD'S NAME

KAY ARTHUR

WATERBROOK
PRESS

THE PEACE AND POWER OF KNOWING GOD'S NAME
PUBLISHED BY WATERBROOK PRESS
2375 Telstar Drive, Suite 160
Colorado Springs, Colorado 80920
A division of Random House, Inc.

All Scripture quotations, unless otherwise indicated, are taken from the *New American Standard Bible*® (NASB).
© Copyright The Lockman Foundation 1960, 1962, 1963, 1968, 1971, 1972, 1973, 1975, 1977.
Used by permission. (www.Lockman.org). Scripture quotations marked (KJV) are taken from the *King James Version.*

Italics in Scripture quotations reflect the author's added emphasis.

ISBN 1-57856-550-2

Copyright © 2002 by Kay Arthur

Interior design by David Carlson Design

Previously published under the title *To Know Him By Name,* copyright © 1995 by Kay Arthur. Material adapted from *Lord, I Want to Know You,* copyright © 1992, 2000 by Kay Arthur.

All rights reserved. No part of this book may be reproduced or transmitted in any form or by any means, electronic or mechanical, including photocopying and recording, or by any information storage and retrieval system, without permission in writing from the publisher.

WATERBROOK and its deer design logo are registered trademarks of WaterBrook Press, a division of Random House, Inc.

Library of Congress Cataloging-in-Publication Data
Arthur, Kay, 1933–
    [To know Him by name]
    The peace & power of knowing God's name / Kay Arthur.—1st WaterBrook Press ed.
       p. cm.
    ISBN 1-57856-550-2
    1. God—Name. I. Title: Peace and power of knowing God's name. II. Title.
    BT180.N2 A635 2002
    231—dc21   2002008687

Printed in the United States of America
2002—First WaterBrook Press Edition

10 9 8 7 6 5 4 3 2 1

CONTENTS

EMMAUS PUBLIC LIBRARY
11 EAST MAIN STREET
EMMAUS, PA 18049

THE NAMES OF THE LORD

*M*y friend tells the story of something that happened while his dad was deer hunting in the wilds of Oregon.

Cradling his rifle in the crook of his arm, his dad was following an old logging road nearly overgrown by the encroaching forest. It was early evening, and he was just thinking about returning to camp when a noise exploded in the brush nearby. Before he even had a chance to lift his rifle, a small blur of brown and white came shooting up the road straight for him.

My friend laughs as he tells the story.

"It all happened so fast, Dad hardly had time to think. He looked down and there was a little brown cottontail—utterly spent—crowded up against his legs between his boots. The little thing was trembling all over, but it just sat there and didn't budge.

"Now this was really strange. Wild rabbits are frightened of people, and it's not often that you'd ever actually *see* one—let alone have one come and sit at your feet.

"While Dad was puzzling over this, another player entered the scene. Down the road—maybe twenty yards away—a weasel burst out of the brush. When it saw my dad—and its intended prey sitting at his feet—the predator froze in its tracks, its mouth panting, its eyes glowing red.

"It was then Dad understood he had stepped into a little life-and-death drama of the forest. The cottontail, exhausted by the chase, was only moments from death. Dad was its last hope of refuge. Forgetting its natural fear and caution, the little animal instinctively crowded up against him for protection from the sharp teeth of its relentless enemy."

My friend's father did not disappoint. He raised his powerful rifle and deliberately shot into the ground just underneath the weasel. The animal seemed to leap almost straight into the air a couple of feet and then rocketed back into the forest just as fast as its legs could move.

For a while, the rabbit didn't stir. It just sat there, huddled at the man's feet in the gathering twilight while he spoke gently to it.

"Where did he go, little one? I don't think he'll be bothering you for a while. Looks like you're off the hook tonight."

Soon the rabbit hopped away from its protector into the forest.

Where, Beloved, do *you* run in time of need?

Where do you run when the predators of trouble, worry, and fear pursue you?

Where do you hide when your past pursues you like a relentless wolf, seeking your destruction?

Where do you seek protection when the weasels of temptation, corruption, and evil threaten to overtake you?

Where do you turn when your energy is spent… when weakness saps you, and you feel you cannot run away any longer?

Do you turn to your Protector, the One who stands with arms open wide, waiting for you to come and huddle in the security of all He is?

The name of the LORD is a strong tower;
The righteous runs into it and is safe.
 (Proverbs 18:10)

Is the Lord your strong tower? Is His name your fortress in a time of weariness or attack or great distress?

But how, you ask, could His *name* defend me? In biblical times, a name represented a person's character. God's name represents His attributes, His nature. His name is a statement of who He is. And He has many names! Each reveals something of His power and love and purposes toward you.

The Father longs to have you know Him better, that you might "trust in the name of the LORD and rely" on your God (Isaiah 50:10).

Did you know that this was uppermost in the mind and heart of Jesus as He faced the Cross? Just before He went to Calvary, He prayed for His disciples—and looking down through the centuries, He prayed for you and me, too. His deep desire was "that they might know thee the only true God, and Jesus Christ, whom thou hast sent" (John 17:3, KJV).

This was the burning goal of Paul's life and the cry of his heart, "that I may know Him" (Philippians 3:10).

Knowing your God means everything. *Everything.*

It's the difference between victory and defeat.

It's the difference between rest and constant turmoil.

It's the difference between an abundant, overflowing life and a life of barren emptiness.

It's the difference between deliverance and captivity.

It's the difference between finding a refuge and living as a fugitive.

It's the difference between life and death.

It's the difference between heaven and hell.

David wrote:

Some boast in chariots, and some in horses;
But we will boast in the name of the LORD, our
    God. (Psalm 20:7)

In Old Testament days, chariots and horses were two means of protection and escape. Today our chariots and horses come with different labels, shapes, and forms. Even so, they are still a visible means of help, escape, or protection. Yet are these really a source of safety? No.

The horse is prepared against the day of battle:
But safety is of the LORD. (Proverbs 21:31, KJV)

Why don't we turn to Him? Why do we hesitate to run to the arms of our all-sufficient God? Why is it that many collapse in the day of trouble and testing? Why are they immobilized rather than taking an aggressive stand in the face of fear?

I think it's because most of us don't really *know* our God. We don't understand His great power and might. We don't comprehend His fierce love and unspeakable tenderness. And because we don't know Him as we should, we can't boast in the name of our God.

What do I mean when I say, "Boast in the name of our God"? *To boast in* means "to have confidence in, to trust in." To boast in God's name means to have confidence in His name. To know His name is to know Him. To boast in His name is to have a settled confidence in everything that He is!

In the day of trouble or need, we are to *run* to our God, to put the full weight of our trust in Him. That is why He says,

Call upon me in the day of trouble: I will deliver thee, and thou shalt glorify me. (Psalm 50:15, KJV)

Is your heart troubled? Is fear lurking in the shadows of your consciousness? Do you ever feel like a little rabbit being chased to exhaustion and despair by a relentless, sharp-toothed weasel? Do you feel insecure about anything at all? With every fiber of my being I believe that every problem in our lives can be traced back to an inadequate or incorrect knowledge of God, or to a lack of faith and trust in His person and His ways. We know so little of this wonderful God who loves us! For the next few pages, as we explore His Word together, ask Him to show you one of His names that will meet your need.

Then, when He shows you (and He will), tell Him that you will *boast* in that name!

With that kind of boasting, God is well pleased.

Is the Lord your strong tower? Is His name your fortress
in a time of weariness or attack or great distress?

CHAPTER ONE

ELOHIM

The Creator

Worthy art Thou, our Lord and our God, to receive glory and honor and power;
for Thou didst create all things, and because of Thy will they existed,
and were created.

REVELATION 4:11

*I*magine you and I are meeting for the first time.

Someone introduces us, and I say, "Hello, I'm Kay." And you reply, "So good to meet you, Kay. I'm Carol (or Constance or Carl)."

One of the first things that you and I ever learn about each other when we are introduced is our first names.

What, then do we learn about God when we first meet Him in Scripture?

Does God have a first name?

Perhaps not. Not like you and I do. But He does have a name that was used *first*.

The very first time you and I meet God in the pages of the Bible, we are introduced to Him by name.

And His name, in the Hebrew language, is *Elohim*.

In the beginning God [Elohim] created the
heavens and the earth. (Genesis 1:1)

Elohim is the name for God, as Creator, in this most foundational passage. It is also the primary word translated "God" throughout the pages of the Old Testament.

But what is that to us? How can the name Elohim serve as a strong tower to us? How can we hide in its depths from the savage storms that sweep into our lives? How does learning this "first name" of God bring us the kind of security and comfort and hope our hearts long for? Is this, after all, just some kind of interesting word study—some elaborate version of "Bible Trivia"?

No! Learning who God is *by name* is the answer to every situation in life. When we know His names, we begin to grapple with His power, His purpose, and His incomparable love.

What does it mean, then, for you and me to encounter Elohim in that first sentence of our Bibles?

El means "mighty" or "strong" and is used for any reference to gods, including Almighty God. The *him* ending of Elohim is very significant, for it is a plural ending in the Hebrew that indicates "more than one." Genesis 1:1 could accurately be translated, "In the beginning Gods created the heavens and the earth."

What? More than one God? No!

"The LORD [Jehovah] is our God [Elohim], the LORD is one!" (Deuteronomy 6:4). God the Father, God the Son, and God the Holy Spirit—the blessed Trinity—created the heavens and the earth. One in essence, in character, yet three persons united as one.

As you read various scriptures, you can see references to the different persons of the Godhead participating in the work of creation.

In Genesis 1:2-3 we read:

The Spirit of God was moving over the surface of the waters. Then God said, "Let there be light"; and there was light.

The writer of Hebrews adds this testimony:

By faith we understand that the worlds were prepared by the word of God. (Hebrews 11:3)

God spoke, the Spirit moved, and Colossians 1:16 tells us that in Him, in Jesus Christ, the Son of God, "all things were created, both in the heavens and on earth." Each person of the triune Godhead had a part in creation. And it was no different when God scooped up the soil of His new world to form the first man. Genesis 1:26 tells us, "Then God [Elohim] said, 'Let Us make man in *Our* image.' "

The "Our" has to refer to more than one! God the Father, God the Son, and God the Holy Spirit were involved in creation. *Your* creation.

Don't skip past that thought. Take a moment to think about it.

God is your Creator.

You exist because of God.

You are the unique and distinctive handiwork of Elohim.

In a moment, in a miracle, you became a living, eternal soul, housed in a body of His design.

So then—

—if you've ever struggled with your self-image…

—if you've ever wept over your family of origin…

—if you've ever bitterly resented who your mother was, or who your father was…

—if you've ever agonized over your reflection in the mirror, or with your physical limitations…

Learning who God is by name is the answer to every situation in life.

Yes, He created the heavens and the earth. He formed the swirling galaxies and the blazing stars and the orbiting planets, and all the life that swarms across the face of our world or swims in the great seas. But He also formed *you*. Specifically. Individually. Thoughtfully. Carefully. Precisely the way you are. God was there when that one particular sperm cell met that one particular egg.

the name of Elohim is your strong tower and unshakable refuge. When you learn to boast in your Elohim, no matter what, life will change!

Scripture tells us that "all things have been created through Him and for Him" (Colossians 1:16). Why were we created? And why were we created precisely the way we are? For Him!

The words of a familiar song ask, *Why was I born? Why am I living?*

Those are more than words to a song, aren't they? They are the heart's cry of every human being who seeks to know the reason for his or her existence. Why were you born? Why did Elohim create you? Search out the answers to these questions, and you will know the purpose for your life.

David wrote:

For Thou didst form my inward parts;
Thou didst weave me in my mother's womb.
I will give thanks to Thee, for I am fearfully
  and wonderfully made;
Wonderful are Thy works,
And my soul knows it very well.
My frame was not hidden from Thee,
When I was made in secret,
And skillfully wrought... (Psalm 139:13-15)

Have you ever thought of yourself as being fearfully and wonderfully made? Carefully, lovingly designed and constructed by an infinitely wise God? Or—if you were very honest—do you look at yourself and despise what Elohim has created?

The truth is, your face may never grace a magazine cover. You may never be asked to model for a television commercial. You may never feel confident standing before a group giving your testimony. You may not be beautiful or exquisite in the eyes of the world. But I can tell you this, Beloved...

Your conception, no matter what the circumstances, was no "accident."

You are exactly as Elohim designed you to be.

He formed the swirling galaxies and the blazing stars and the orbiting planets.... But He also formed you.

And that design has a purpose.

And that purpose is to bring God glory.

I have a friend who is probably not more than three feet tall. Her head is of normal size, and to me she is lovely. Yet Julie spends all her days in a sling, much like a baby's walker. In order for her to move anywhere, her legs must push the rolling frame. Julie is radiant, a delight to all who meet her. She knows her Elohim! And she clings to the truth that He created her this way for a purpose. Now, please don't tell me God had nothing to do with her physical condition. If so, I must deny His sovereignty, His Word, and His name.

Remember when Moses said to the Lord, "Please, Lord, I have never been eloquent, neither recently nor in time past, nor since Thou hast spoken to Thy servant; for I am slow of speech and slow of tongue" (Exodus 4:10).

And what was the Lord's reply?

Who has made man's mouth? Or who makes him dumb or deaf, or seeing or blind? Is it not I, the LORD? (Exodus 4:11)

But why would God create people who are different from His normal pattern of creation? Why would He ever permit a human conception when it would produce what seems to be a genetic disaster?

The disciples had the same question in mind when they encountered the man who had been blind from birth. They asked the Lord, "Rabbi, who sinned, this man or his parents, that he should be born blind?" (John 9:2).

How did Jesus answer?

"It was neither that this man sinned, nor his parents; but it was in order that the works of God might be displayed in him" (John 9:3).

You are exactly as Elohim designed you to be. And that design has a purpose.

Oh, Beloved, if you are not happy with your-self…with your past…with your limitations…with the heartbreaking limitations of your child or loved one, run into the strong tower of the name of your Elohim (Proverbs 18:10). You may not understand how your situation could *ever* bring Him glory, but He doesn't ask or require you to understand. He simply asks you to trust in the name of your Lord.

Who is among you that fears the LORD,
That obeys the voice of His servant,
That walks in darkness and has no light?
Let him trust in the name of the LORD and rely
    on his God. (Isaiah 50:10)

The prophet recorded these words:

Thus says the LORD, your Creator, O Jacob,
And He who formed you, O Israel…
"I am the LORD your God [Elohim]…
You are precious in My sight…
Everyone who is called by My name,
And whom I have created for My glory,
Whom I have formed, even whom I have
    made." (Isaiah 43:1,3-4,7)

According to Isaiah 43, Elohim, the One who made man, male and female, in His image, created you for His glory.

One day while studying what God's Word says about the husband-wife relationship, I decided that since "woman is the glory of man" (1 Corinthians 11:7), I had better look up the meaning of the word *glory*. It means "to give the correct opinion or estimate of." I saw that as a woman I am to treat my husband in such a way as to give a correct opinion or estimate of him as a man.

Can you see how awesome it is to know that you have been created for God's glory? That you are to live in such a way as to give all of creation a correct opin-ion or estimate of who God is? What does that mean to you, O child of God, who is called by His name? Think about it. How would you live if you were to live for His glory?

Let me show you one other scripture that tells you why you were born.

> Worthy art Thou, our Lord and our God, to receive glory and honor and power; for Thou didst create all things, and because of Thy will they existed, and were created. (Revelation 4:11)

According to this scripture, you were created for His will. The *King James Version* says "pleasure." In essence, they are the same. If I live for His will, that is His pleasure, or if I bring Him pleasure, it is because I have done His will.

His Name is Elohim.

Almighty God.

Your Creator.

You were created for His glory and for His pleasure. Your life is to be lived in such a way as to reflect Him, to show the world the character of God—His love, His peace, His mercy, His gentleness. You are to live for Him, to accomplish His will. To miss this is to miss fulfillment. It is to have existed rather than to have lived.

Go before your God and evaluate the course of your life. Are you fulfilling the purpose of your creation? What is keeping you from being or doing what you were created for? What do you need to change? What do you need to do? Will you? Answer these questions honestly in His presence.

To know your Elohim is to know your very reason for drawing breath.

You may spend the rest of your life experiencing the wonder of God's "first name."

You may not understand how your situation could ever bring Him glory,

but He doesn't ask or require you to understand.

He simply asks you to trust in the name of your Lord. ✿

CHAPTER TWO

EL ELYON

The God Most High

I am God, and there is no other; I am God, and there is no one like Me,

My purpose will be established,

And I will accomplish all My good pleasure.

ISAIAH 46:9-10

God's name, His first name in Scripture, is Elohim, *our* Elohim. And we could spend the balance of our days—on into eternity—pondering the height and the breadth and the depth of that name.

But He has another name, too. A wonderful name. A surpassingly powerful name.

Of all the names of God, no other name means as much to me as this one.

It is a name that has sustained me through every trial and storm of my life.

It is a name that has enabled me to live with my past.

It is a name that empowers me to face whatever may lie in my future.

It is the strongest of strong towers.

El Elyon—God Most High.

It is one thing to know that God created the earth. But what then? Did He wind it up like a clock and walk away from it? Is He involved? Can God protect what He created? Can He sustain what His great mind conceived and His great hand set in motion? Can He fulfill His purposes for His creation? He made me and gave me life, but is He strong enough and wise enough to touch the individual moments of my day? Is He aware and involved enough to help me deal with life *right now*?

Yes. There can be no doubt. He is God Most High.

El Elyon is the name that designates God as the sovereign Ruler of all the universe.

It was Abraham, the friend of God, to whom this mighty name was first revealed in Scripture. The old patriarch, known then as Abram, had just returned from an astounding rout of four powerful armies. With 318 men of his own household, Abram defeated four kings, released those taken captive, and recovered his plundered goods.

Three hundred eighteen men against *four armies*? One elderly nomad against a military alliance of four oriental kings in all their pomp and splendor? Something supernatural was going on here, and Abram was no fool. He knew that a power higher than that of kings rode with his little war band. Who after all was Tidal, "King of Nations," against God Most High? Who were Amraphel king of Shinar, Arioch king of Ellasar, Chedorlaomer king of Elam alongside the Possessor of heaven and earth?

Here, then, is our first encounter with El Elyon.

Then after his return from the defeat of Chedorlaomer and the kings who were with him, the king of Sodom went out to meet him at the valley of Shaveh (that is, the King's Valley). And Melchizedek king of Salem brought out bread and wine; now he was a priest of [El Elyon] God Most High. And he blessed him and said,

"Blessed be Abram of God Most High,
Possessor of heaven and earth;
And blessed be God Most High,
Who has delivered your enemies into your
    hand." (Genesis 14:17-20)

Later, when the king of Sodom tried to reward Abram, the patriarch replied,

If you will bow your knee to the all-embracing sovereignty of the Most High God, then you will experience a deep and abiding peace.

I have sworn to the LORD God Most High,
possessor of heaven and earth, that I will not
take a thread or a sandal thong or anything that
is yours, lest you should say, "I have made
Abram rich." (Genesis 14:22-23)

It was El Elyon who had given Abram the victory. It was the Most High God who was and is the Redeemer of Israel, Abraham's descendants (Psalm 78:35). And it is the Most High God who rules today over the affairs of men. How did that mighty king of old state it?

Nebuchadnezzar…blessed [El Elyon] the Most
High and praised and honored Him who lives
forever…
"His dominion is an everlasting dominion,
And His kingdom endures from generation to
generation.
And all the inhabitants of the earth are accounted
as nothing,

But He does according to His will in the host
of heaven
And among the inhabitants of earth;
And no one can ward off His hand
Or say to Him, 'What has Thou done?' "
(Daniel 4:34-35)

The king of Babylon uttered those words of praise after seven years of insanity had robbed him of his throne, his dignity, and his very humanity. At the end of those years, the naked, bestial king lifted his eyes toward the heavens. And the first thought to pierce the profound darkness of his deranged mind was this:

God Most High rules over all.

With that single thought, light flooded his mind, sanity returned, and he reclaimed his throne.

So it is with us. The unshakable fact of God's sovereign control over all is the foundation of sanity in this crazy world. It is the truth that gives stability and order and ultimate hope in the midst of maddening circumstances. I have known men and women to nearly lose their minds by refusing to acknowledge His absolute sovereignty over the affairs of life.

Listen carefully, Beloved. If God is not sovereign, if He is not in control, if all things are not under His dominion, then He is *not* the Most High, and you and I are either in the hands of blind fate, in the hands of man, or in the hands of the devil.

But Scripture leaves no doubt, no shadow of misgiving. Hear the words of a sovereign God, a God who never hesitates or stutters:

The LORD of hosts has sworn saying, "Surely, just as I have intended so it has happened, and just as I have planned so it will stand… For the LORD of hosts has planned, and who can frustrate it? And as for His stretched-out hand, who can turn it back?" (Isaiah 14:24,27)

Remember the former things long past,
For I am God, and there is no other;
I am God, and there is no one like Me,
Declaring the end from the beginning
And from ancient times things which have
    not been done,
Saying, "My purpose will be established,
And I will accomplish all My good pleasure";
Calling a bird of prey from the east,
The man of My purpose from a far country.
Truly I have spoken; truly I will bring it to pass.
I have planned it, surely I will do it.
    (Isaiah 46:9-11)

The unshakable fact of God's sovereign control over all is the foundation of sanity in this crazy world.

What difference does it make in your life when you realize God is sovereign, that He is Ruler over all, and that *nothing* can happen without the ultimate sanction or permission of God?

I can only tell you this: If you begin to grasp the depth of the name El Elyon, if you will submit to that name, if you will bow your knee to the all-embracing sovereignty of the Most High God, then you will

verse can touch your life except by His permission and filtered through His fingers of love.

The truth of God's sovereignty makes it easier to obey those commands in the New Testament that charge us to rejoice in all circumstances of life. God tells us that we are to "be filled with the Spirit…always giving thanks for all things in the name of our Lord Jesus Christ to God, even the Father" (Ephesians 5:18,20).

El Elyon, God Most High, is in control and nothing can happen across His wide universe without His permission.

experience a deep and abiding peace in the very core of your being that defies description. You can know with certainty that nothing occurs in the world of angels, in the world of demons, in the world of men, or in your own daily world that does not fall under His control. You will know that nothing in the uni-

Doesn't this become easier when you know that your Father, El Elyon, God Most High, is in control and that nothing can happen across His wide universe without His permission?

When we are misunderstood or slandered by others, we can still give thanks.

When we are deliberately harmed or wronged by others, we can still give thanks.

When we are shunned or ignored or devalued by others, we can still give thanks.

Although we have been given a free will, God so rules and overrules in this universe of His that no person, angel, demon, or devil—nor any circumstance of life—can thwart His plan.

El Elyon rules supremely over all. And because He does, you can understand how all things "work together for good to those who love God, to those who are called according to His purpose" (Romans 8:28). In everything you can "give thanks; for this is God's will for you in Christ Jesus" (1 Thessalonians 5:18).

Do you remember how Joseph's brothers plotted his demise? Because of his brothers' jealousy, Joseph was stripped of his cherished cloak, thrown into a pit, then sold to be a slave in Egypt. There, in the house of Potiphar, he was falsely accused and unjustly imprisoned for two long, weary years.

It was enough to make any normal man bitter at God. Joseph had done what was right, had been faithful to his God, and suffered because of it. He seemed the victim of the whims and plots of men. And yet not once during all this time did Joseph do anything but honor his God (Genesis 39:9; 40:8; 41:25,28).

Why? Because this young man saw something through the eyes of faith. He saw El Elyon, the Most High God, standing in the shadows, ruling over all, watching and waiting. Whether or not he understood everything that happened to him, Joseph knew that God had a purpose in it all. How can I say that? Because of what Joseph said to his brothers when they found themselves standing before him as the appointed ruler over all Egypt (Genesis 42:6).

Listen to the words of a man who had been terribly wronged—who had endured wounds as deep as you and I will ever experience. Yet hear the words of a man who knew how to find refuge and strength and perspective in the high, strong tower of El Elyon.

And now do not be grieved or angry with yourselves, because you sold me here; for God sent me before you to preserve life.... And God sent me before you to preserve for you a remnant in the earth, and to keep you alive by a great deliverance. Now, therefore, it was not you who sent me here, but God; and He has made me a father to Pharaoh and lord of all his household and ruler over all the land of Egypt....

And as for you, you meant evil against me, but God meant it for good in order to bring about this present result, to preserve many people alive. (Genesis 45:5,7-8; 50:20)

"You meant evil against me, but God meant it for good! God used your every action, intended to hurt and wound and exploit, to bring about His great life-giving, nation-shaping plan!"

What a God! *God Most High.*

O Beloved, the next time you start to murmur or complain, run to your El Elyon, trust in His name, and give thanks. Bend your knee before God Most High, and learn that His sovereign power toward you means nothing less than perfect love.

El Elyon rules supremely over all.

And because He does, you can understand how all things

"work together for good to those who love God,

to those who are called according to His purpose."

CHAPTER THREE

EL ROI

The God Who Sees

For the ways of a man are before the eyes of the LORD,
And He watches all his paths.

PROVERBS 5:21

*T*hrown out!

Like a soiled, worthless rag.

Used for another's pleasure and then tossed aside. It was too much. It was more than she could handle. Feeling like an outcast, she bundled a few of her things together and headed out the door, vowing never to return.

That's one "day in the life" of Hagar, the maid of Sarai and the one who bore the son of Sarai's husband, Abram.

Have you ever known such a day in your life? Have you ever known what it means to be thrown out, completely rejected? You fulfilled someone's pleasure—and then you weren't wanted anymore! Did you run away? Were you put out on the street?

Did you find yourself wondering if there was some way in which you failed or were inadequate? Maybe if you had behaved differently, maybe if you had been more than you were, maybe if you had… The speculations go on and on, don't they?

People tell you that it wasn't your fault. That you weren't the only one in the wrong. But right or wrong, you feel the rejection deep inside, and with rejection comes that crushing feeling of inadequacy.

Where is God? you ask. *Where is Elohim, the Creator-God who designed me for His will and His purposes? Where is El Elyon, this sovereign God who promises that all things work together for good? Does He really know what's going on? Does He see?*

Yes. He sees.

It is His very name.

He is *El Roi*—The God Who Sees.

The omnipresent God is there, and His eyes are not shut. He isn't asleep, He isn't caught off guard, and He isn't hindered by the darkness.

God sees!

Hagar discovered this soon after she fled from the tense situation in her home. Thirsty, probably lonely and exhausted, she eventually threw herself down by a spring of water in the desert wilderness. Where would she go? What would she do? What would become of her? What would happen to the child she carried in her womb?

It was a big, empty world in those ancient days. And an utterly frightening one for a young, pregnant slave girl with broken family ties and no prospects.

It's not too difficult to imagine Hagar weeping her heart out by that little spring in a wild, barren land. She had no doubt heard Abram speak of this El Elyon—this powerful, "possessor of heaven and earth." Where was He now? Did He care about someone as lowly as a servant girl? Did He see her in her grief and great distress?

Just about that time, as she pondered these things, Hagar had a visitor.

> Now the angel of the LORD found her by a spring of water in the wilderness, by the spring on the way to Shur. And he said, "Hagar, Sarai's maid, where have you come from and where are you going?" And she said, "I am fleeing from the presence of my mistress Sarai." (Genesis 16:7-8)

This was none other than the Lord Himself, in the form of an angel. How can I say that? Because He speaks

The omnipresent God is there, and His eyes are not shut.... God sees! 🖋

as the Lord in verse 10. He says, "I will greatly multiply your descendants…."

And Hagar, like another desolate woman at another well millennia later, discovers some amazing things about God in those moments by the spring.

He knows right where to find her.

He knows her name.

He knows her occupation.

He knows her heartaches at home.

He knows about the child in her womb—what his name will be, and what kind of man he will become.

What is more, He knows her future…He knows her destiny.

How awed and amazed that little maid must have been! Listen to her response:

Then she called the name of the LORD who spoke to her, "Thou art a God who sees"; for she said, "Have I even remained alive here after seeing Him?" Therefore the well was called Beer-lahai-roi [the well of the living one who sees me]. (Genesis 16:13-14)

The Lord had said to her, "Where have you come from and where are you going?" There was concern for Hagar's past and her future in that question. It was as if the Lord was saying, "Where have you been, Hagar? What has hurt you? Why are you running? What will happen to you if you keep running and running like this?"

Many times when we are mistreated, used by someone we trusted or respected, we tend to run away from

Can any abused person, any person used for another's perverted pleasure, ever be whole? Yes, healing has to be possible. Otherwise, a sovereign God of love would surely have intervened.

the situation—or we seek to bury it. The memory of it, the emotions, the rejection all seem too much to bear, so we "stuff it." I guess we think that if we stuff it, it will go away.

had stuffed it. Run away from it. Covered it over. Some even wondered if they were dreaming. How could anything so unnatural, so horrible be real? But they knew they weren't dreaming.

Where does healing begin? It begins with recognition of El Roi. It begins with the God who sees.

But our computer-like memory bank stores it. Then something happens, and the program is called up and replayed on the screen of our memory. The pain, the bitterness, the recriminations are too much—so once again, it's stuffed.

Some time ago I did five television programs on incest. The mail flooded in for weeks afterward, and it wasn't easy mail to read. I wept. I hurt. I was horrified. How could people do things like this to one another? Many people told their story for the first time. Years had passed, yet for most there had been no healing. They

How could they ever be whole? Can any abused person, any person used for another's perverted pleasure, ever be whole? Whether it be sexual, mental, or physical abuse, can there be healing? Yes, healing has to be possible. Otherwise, a sovereign God of love would surely have intervened.

But where does healing begin?

It begins with recognition of El Roi.

It begins with the God who sees.

He was awake. He was aware. He saw it all.

The first time we meet God in the Word as El Roi,

we find Him telling Hagar to go back and *deal* with the situation.

> Then the angel of the LORD said to her, "Return to your mistress, and submit yourself to her authority." (Genesis 16:9)

If you have been a victim of incest or abuse—or any other injustice—you need to get it out, face it, and deal with what happened as it really was. God saw it all—there is no hiding the facts from Him, "for the ways of a man are before the eyes of the LORD, and He watches all his paths" (Proverbs 5:21).

God sees all. He knows the sin that was committed against you. And someday, Beloved, He will vindicate you. There is forgiveness, but to those who refuse to receive the Lamb of God who takes away the sins of the world, there is also a day of judgment. And it will be a righteous judgment, for God's gaze misses nothing (2 Thessalonians 1:5-10).

After you realize that He sees, you need to know that in His sovereignty He *permitted* what happened. Therefore, as horrible and as destructive as it seems, in God's economy it will be used for good if you will but know Him, believe Him, and put your trust in His name. For He does not forsake those who seek Him (Psalm 9:10).

That is one way it helps to know His name El Roi. Let me mention another.

If you have loved ones who have run away or cut themselves off from communication, you may have no

Where is El Elyon, this sovereign God who promises that all things work together for good? Does He really know what's going on? Does He see? Yes. He sees. It is His very name.

idea where they are or what is happening in their lives.

But El Roi does.

He knows where they have come from and where they are going. He knows what they are thinking and feeling in the deepest part of their hearts.

He sees it all. Right now. *At this very instant.*

You can't, but He can.

God sees all. He knows the sin that was committed against you.

And someday, Beloved, He will vindicate you. ✒

We recently received a letter at Precept Ministries telling the story of a woman who ran into the tower of El Roi—and found Him true to His name. Darlene had spent many years in a women's correctional facility in Arkansas. She began attending a Precept class there in prison and found herself deeply touched by a study on the names of God. The week her class

studied El Roi was very moving to her. She wrote the name down on a slip of paper and carried it with her everywhere.

Darlene had been sentenced to a long prison term while her little boy was still in elementary school. She had not seen him for many years but had learned that as a teenager, he had become involved with gangs and

drugs. At the age of sixteen, he had run away from his father's home…and had not been heard from since.

Darlene, however, never stopped thinking about him as the long years slipped by…worrying about him, longing for him. If he was still alive, he would be twenty-seven years old. Darlene knew he was most likely dead. But still, while there was hope, she prayed.

Every time she became anxious about her son, she pulled the slip of paper from her pocket and thought about the name she had written there.

El Roi…The God Who Sees.

God knew where her son was, even if she didn't. God could see him…and perhaps He would have mercy on a broken-hearted mother and allow her to see her boy again.

Within a few weeks of the study on El Roi—while the prison group was still studying the names of God together—Darlene received a phone call from a hospital in Texas. Her son was alive. He had been having mental problems from his extensive drug use and was under treatment. Somehow, the hospital had been able to track down the man's mother, in an Arkansas prison.

Then they put him on the line, and this dear woman spoke with her son for the first time in many long years.

She had the name El Roi in her pocket, and in her heart. He had seen her in her need, and He had been merciful.

You can trust Him, too, Beloved. You *must* trust Him. He alone is absolutely trustworthy.

Run into the strong fortress of His name—and rest.

You can trust Him. He alone is absolutely trustworthy.

Run into the strong fortress of His name—and rest.

CHAPTER FOUR

EL SHADDAI

The All-Sufficient One

*Whoever drinks of the water that I shall give him shall never thirst;
but the water that I shall give him shall become in him a
well of water springing up to eternal life.*

JOHN 4:14

*W*hen Abram first heard the name, it put him flat on his face. It was a most appropriate place to meet God Almighty. It was a most appropriate moment for God to reveal Himself as *El Shaddai.*

This is how it happened:

Now when Abram was ninety-nine years old,
the LORD appeared to Abram and said to him,

"I am God Almighty [El Shaddai];
Walk before Me, and be blameless.
And I will establish My covenant between Me
    and you,
And I will multiply you exceedingly."

And Abram fell on his face, and God talked with him, saying,

"As for Me, behold, My covenant is with you,
And you shall be the father of a multitude of
    nations.
No longer shall your name be called Abram,
But your name shall be Abraham;
For I will make you the father of a multitude of
    nations.

And I will make you exceedingly fruitful, and I will make nations of you, and kings shall come forth from you. And I will establish My covenant between Me and you and your descendants after you throughout their generations for an everlasting covenant, to be God to you and to your descendants after you. And I will give to you and to your descendants after you, the land of your sojournings, all the land of Canaan, for an everlasting possession; and I will be their God." (Genesis 17:1-8)

God appeared to Abram, and the old man fell on his face.

What did God say to him?

"I am God Almighty.... I am El Shaddai. Walk before Me, and be blameless, and I will establish My covenant with you." In other words, *I am your all-sufficient One.* Quit running. Quit hiding. Quit seeking other ways. Trust in Me. Rest in Me. Let Me supply your needs.

El, remember, actually stands for might or power. The translation of *Shaddai* is not as clear in its meaning, for scholars differ on the meaning of its root word. Some feel that it speaks of God in His might and power as seen in His judgments. I lean toward a definition set forth clearly by Andrew Jukes in *The Names of God:*

> The thought expressed in the name "Shaddai"... describes power, but it is the power, not of violence, but of all-bountifulness. "Shaddai" primarily means "Breasted," being formed directly from the Hebrew word *Shad,* that is, "the breast," or, more exactly, a "woman's breast." Parkhurst thus explains the name—"Shaddai, one of the Divine titles, meaning *The Pourer* or *Shedder forth,* that is, of blessings, temporal and spiritual...."

When I have run to Him, I have never come away wanting.

He is my El Shaddai, my all-sufficient One.

I need hardly explain how this title, "Breasted," or "Pourer-forth," came to mean "Almighty." Mothers at least will understand it.

A babe is crying—restless. Nothing can quiet it. Yes: The breast can.

A babe is pining—starving. Its life is ebbing away. It cannot take man's proper food; it will die. No. The breast can give it fresh life, nourishment. By her breast the mother has almost infinite power over the child.

This is El Shaddai, the "Pourer-forth," who pours Himself out for His creatures; who gives them His lifeblood; who "sheds forth His Spirit" and says, "Come unto me and drink…. Open thy mouth wide, and I will fill it." This is the God who, by the sacrifice of Himself, gives Himself and His very nature to those who will receive Him.

If anyone needed to know God as El Shaddai, it was Abraham. He was ninety-nine years old, and Sarah was eighty-nine, and still they were childless. Yet God had promised them a child of their own. Scripture tells us: "And without becoming weak in faith he contemplated his own body, now as good as dead since he was about a hundred years old, and the deadness of Sarah's womb" (Romans 4:19).

Abraham thought about the deadness of his reproductive powers. He considered the deadness of Sarah's womb. And even though he knew perfectly well that zero plus zero does not equal one, he factored another element into the equation.

How could Abraham give glory to God in such a seemingly hopeless situation?

It was because he had met El Shaddai.

When I was twenty-nine, on my knees beside my bed, I met my El Shaddai.

Time and time again I have found Him to be my all-sufficient God. My Protector. The unconditional Lover of my soul.

He held me through my divorce.

He held me through the suicide of my first husband.

He held me as a single parent overwhelmed by loneliness and the crush of responsibility.

He has held me through times of great financial need.

He has held me when the pains of leadership seemed overwhelming.

He has held me when I have failed.

He has held me when I have wept for my children and doubted myself as a mother.

He has held me when I have had no more strength and wondered how I would ever make it.

He has held me when I felt overwhelmed by all that I had to do.

When I have run to Him, I have never come away wanting. He is my El Shaddai, my all-sufficient One. God Almighty.

O Beloved, do you understand? Have you experienced Him as your El Shaddai? If not, He is waiting, arms open wide for you.

He is the One who delights to succor His people.

He is the One who delights to comfort His children.

He is the One who longs to hold and protect His own. Hear the words of El Shaddai:

Can a woman forget her nursing child,
And have no compassion on the son of her womb?
Even these may forget, but I will not forget you.
Behold, I have inscribed you on the palms of
    My hands. (Isaiah 49:15-16)

When I was a little girl—just a skinny little beanpole with pigtails—I used to run to my daddy for comfort. I was a tomboy who consistently fell out of trees,

Time and time again I have found Him to be my all-sufficient God.

My Protector. The unconditional Lover of my soul.

got into fights, and crashed my bicycle. It seemed as if I was forever bloodying these poor banged-up knees of mine. That's when I would run—with pigtails flying and dirty tears streaming down my face—to my daddy.

"Daddy! Daddy! Daddy!"

Many years later I was hurting again, so very deeply.

But I couldn't run to my daddy.

I was a single mom with two little kids, trying to work and go to school. And it was one of those days when everything seemed to catch up with me—all of

This is El Shaddai, the "Pourer-forth," who pours Himself out for His creatures.

And I'm so fortunate, because I had a daddy who held me. Ever since I was a little girl until the day he went to be with the Lord, I was always his sweetheart. And I would fly into his open arms, and he would gather me up on his lap—dirt, blood, and all—and hold me there. And he would wipe away my tears and push back my pigtails, and say, "Now, Honey, tell Daddy all about it."

the hurt and loneliness and regret and pressure and weariness. I remember driving into the driveway of the little brick home where we were living. I got out of the car and began walking down the gravel walkway toward the front door.

For some reason, time seemed to stand still for a moment.

To this day I can't tell you what triggered the thought,

but suddenly—in my mind's eye—I saw something.

I saw a little girl, running.

I saw a little girl with tears streaming down her face and banged-up, bloody knees on those skinny little legs. I saw her in need of her daddy. Running for her daddy.

Then suddenly—strangely—I saw her running down a huge, shiny corridor. A vast corridor with gleaming marble walls and beautiful windows spilling heavenly

And I knew that the little girl was me, and that I was running toward the very throne room of El Elyon, sovereign Ruler of the universe. Yet I was the daughter of the King of kings, so when the guards saw me coming, they swung open those doors and let me run in. There I was, weeping and running into the very presence of El Elyon. I heard the cherubim and the seraphim crying out, "Holy, holy, holy, Lord God Almighty! Heaven and earth are full of Thy glory!" Many bowed before

He is our Rock, our Refuge, our very present help in time of trouble. Everything you and I will ever need can be found in the all-sufficient One, God Almighty. 🌿

light. And at the end of that marble hallway were massive doors of brilliant gold. Standing before those doors were bright, powerful guards with great spears.

the throne, and court was in session, but I just ran and ran and didn't stop. Because the One on the throne was not only Elohim my Creator, not only El Elyon, the sovereign Ruler of the universe, but He was also my El Shaddai, my all-sufficient One.

I could just see myself running up the wide stairs to that glorious throne—two steps at a time—crying "Abba, Father! *Daddy!*"

And I could see Him stopping everything, opening His arms wide and just gathering me to His chest, saying, "There, there, My precious child. Let Me wipe away those tears. Tell your Father all about it."

Weakness and difficulty and need present no problem to El Shaddai 🌿

When I found out that God was my El Shaddai, I knew where to run. The thing I'd always longed for in a man was someone stronger than I was, because I'm a very strong woman. I wanted someone who would put his arms around me and hold me and protect me and keep me. I wanted a place of refuge, a place where I could run when I was hurting or afraid.

And—after all those years of frantic searching—I found that refuge in my El Shaddai.

He is our Rock, our Refuge, our very present help in time of trouble. Everything you and I will ever need can be found in the all-sufficient One, God Almighty.

This is the truth the name El Shaddai proclaims. The truth came home to Abram with his face in the dust before the Almighty. It must have echoed in his mind again and again as he gazed into the face of

baby Isaac and watched his little boy grow strong and sturdy and tall. There were other tests yet to come for the old patriarch—tests that would push him to the utter edge of human endurance. But from that time on he knew where to run for strength.

Many centuries later, Paul would learn the same truth:

And He has said to me, "My grace is sufficient for you, for power is perfected in weakness." Most gladly, therefore, I will rather boast about my weaknesses, that the power of Christ may dwell in me. Therefore I am well content with weaknesses, with insults, with distresses, with persecutions, with difficulties, for Christ's sake; for when I am weak, then I am strong. (2 Corinthians 12:9-10)

Weakness and difficulty and need—*and human impossibilities*—present no problem to El Shaddai.

The Almighty has all the might you could ever require.

Run to Him—run right into the throne room—and find His arms open wide.

CHAPTER FIVE

ADONAI

The Lord

Do you not know that when you present yourselves to someone as slaves for obedience,

you are slaves of the one whom you obey, either of sin resulting in death,

or of obedience resulting in righteousness?

ROMANS 6:16

*B*efore God revealed Himself to Abram as the all-sufficient God Almighty who could meet Abram's every need, there was an earlier encounter.

Before Abram learned of an El Shaddai, he acknowledged God by a different name. And so, I believe, must we. The name is first used in Genesis 15:1-2:

> After these things the word of the LORD came
> to Abram in a vision, saying,

> "Do not fear, Abram,
> I am a shield to you;
> Your reward shall be very great."

And Abram said, "O Lord [Adonai] GOD [Jehovah], what wilt Thou give me, since I am childless?"

After experiencing a great victory against powerful enemies and enormous odds, and after coming to know God as El Elyon, God Most High and Sovereign of the universe, Abram acknowledged God's lordship over his *own* life. Over all that he had and was. Abram, a man with firsthand knowledge of the master-slave relationship, called Him *Adonai.*

Lord.

Master.

Owner.

How well His servants have known that name down through the ages!

Before you can really know God as El Shaddai, the all-sufficient One, I believe you must bow before Him as Adonai, your Lord and Master.

On the day I was saved, I could never have known the refuge of His arms without first bowing my knee and acknowledging His right to rule over me. When I came to Him on July 16, 1963, I said, "Lord, You can do anything You want with me."

Do you see the need to bow before Him and say, "My Lord"?

Do you see the necessity to acknowledge Him as supreme Ruler and Master of all that you are and have?

So many people in churches across our country seem disappointed or bored with their experience of "Christianity." Have you noticed? Somehow the Christian life seems less than what they had expected or hoped for. It doesn't seem to satisfy. It doesn't meet their deepest needs. So, maintaining the outer shell of a "Christian faith," they push aside that nagging feeling of empti-

Acknowledging Him as Lord has to be something more than mere words.

It's a relationship!

On that day of days, I did not know that Adonai was one of His names. But I had come to the place of total commitment to the will of God. And when I acknowledged Him as my Lord, I found my El Shaddai.

ness, and they busily—sometimes frantically—give themselves to other pursuits.

Is it true that God isn't "enough" for some people? Is it true that Christianity just can't satisfy certain men and women? Or could it be that these people have never experienced true Christianity? Could it be that they have never truly bowed the knee to Adonai and owned Him as Lord?

Study the Scriptures that relate to Him as Lord—in both the Old and New Testaments—and then see how you would answer those questions.

Do you remember what Jesus said in His Sermon on the Mount?

> Not everyone who says to Me, "Lord, Lord," will enter the kingdom of heaven; but he who does the will of My Father who is in heaven. Many will say to Me on that day, "Lord, Lord, did we not prophesy in Your name, and in Your name cast out demons, and in Your name perform many miracles?" And then I will declare to them, "I never knew you; depart from Me, you who practice lawlessness." (Matthew 7:21-23)

> Why do you call Me, "Lord, Lord," and do not do what I say? (Luke 6:46)

It's a simple question—but powerful. Acknowledging Him as Lord has to be something more than mere words. It's a relationship! It's where a relationship with God must begin. The lordship of God means His total possession of me and my total submission to Him as Master.

Can a person really be saved and deny God's lordship over his life?

Can a man or woman really call Jesus Christ "Lord" and steadfastly refuse to do the things He tells them to do?

Can you or I really expect eternal life in heaven when we've never bowed before Him as Lord on earth?

Can you or I really expect eternal life in heaven when we've never bowed before Him as Lord on earth?

These are questions that could make all the difference in your understanding of true Christianity. With submission to Him as Lord comes all we need for whatever task He places before us. Whatever it is, Adonai supplies what His servants need in order to perform their Master's will.

But as Adonai, He has a right to expect obedience! Wasn't this why God became angry with Moses in their meeting at the burning bush? God commissioned the old shepherd to go before Pharaoh and secure the release of His people. But listen carefully as Moses replies to God. (As you read, remember that when "LORD" is in capital letters, it is the word *Jehovah;* otherwise the word is *Adonai* or *Adon.*)

Then Moses said to the LORD, "Please, Lord, I have never been eloquent, neither recently nor in time past, nor since Thou has spoken to Thy servant; for I am slow of speech and slow of tongue." And the LORD said to him, "Who has made man's mouth? Or who makes him dumb or deaf, or seeing or blind? Is it not I, the LORD? Now then go, and I, even I, will be with your mouth, and teach you what you are to say." But he said, "Please, Lord, now send the message by whomever Thou wilt." Then the anger of the LORD burned against Moses. (Exodus 4:10-14)

Why was God angry? Because Moses was *saying,* "Lord, Lord...Adonai, Adonai," but he was not trusting and submitting to Him as Adonai. What good does it do to form the word *Lord* with your lips when your knees don't bend in acknowledgment of His lordship and your feet turn away from His chosen paths?

Centuries later the Lord Jesus would survey the religious scene of His day and say with a sigh, "Rightly did Isaiah prophesy of you, saying, 'This people honors Me with their lips, but their heart is far away from Me'" (Matthew 15:7-8).

Where is your heart, Beloved?

If God is God, then He must be Adonai—He must be Master.

If Jesus is God, then He, too, must be Jehovah Adonai. Lord.

Listen carefully to what Jesus taught:

Now great multitudes were going along with Him; and He turned and said to them, "If anyone comes to Me, and does not hate his own father and mother and wife and children and brothers and sisters, yes, and even his own life, he cannot be My disciple. Whoever does not carry his own cross and come after Me cannot be My disciple." (Luke 14:25-27)

Jesus is Master. Jesus is Lord.

So it is that Jude warns us:

Beloved, while I was making every effort to write you about our common salvation, I felt the necessity to write to you appealing that you contend earnestly for the faith which was once for all delivered to the saints. For certain persons have crept in unnoticed, those who were long beforehand marked out for this condemnation, ungodly persons who turn the grace of our God into licentiousness and deny our only Master and Lord, Jesus Christ. (Jude 3-4)

For those who have eyes to see, this is the clear, consistent teaching of the New Testament. Over and over Jesus confronted His hearers with His deity. Many even today don't mind acknowledging Jesus Christ as a good man, or even as a prophet, but they do not want to acknowledge Him as God. For if He is God, then He must be *honored* as God. Every knee must bow and confess Him as Lord to the glory of the Father (Philippians 2:10-11).

> But what does it say? "The word is near you,
> in your mouth and in your heart"—that is,
> the word of faith which we are preaching, that
> if you confess with your mouth Jesus as Lord,
> and believe in your heart that God raised Him
> from the dead, you shall be saved; for with

the heart man believes, resulting in righteousness, and with the mouth he confesses, resulting in salvation. (Romans 10:8-10)

Abram acknowledged God as his Adonai and later found him to be El Shaddai, the all-sufficient One who would nurture him and richly bless him and be to him all that He is.

Yes, He is Master and Lord. But what a Master! What a Lord! And what a joy to bow before the One whose love can never be measured throughout time and eternity.

For if He is God, then He must be honored as God.

CHAPTER SIX

JEHOVAH

The Self-Existent One

Before Me there was no God formed,
And there will be none after Me.
I, even I, am the LORD;
And there is no savior besides Me.

ISAIAH 43:10-11

After forty years of leading sheep around and around in an arid wilderness, most any diversion would have been welcome.

A burning bush? Well, it certainly rated a second look. A bush that went on burning and burning—yet never burned up? Now *that* merited a closer examination!

So Moses said, "I must turn aside now, and see this marvelous sight, why the bush is not burned up." When the LORD saw that he turned aside to look, God called to him from the midst of the bush, and said, "Moses, Moses!" And he said, "Here I am." Then He said, "Do not come near here; remove your san-dals from your feet, for the place on which you are standing is holy ground." He said also, "I am the God of your father, the God of Abraham, the God of Isaac, and the God of Jacob." Then Moses hid his face, for he was afraid to look at God. (Exodus 3:3-6)

It was well that Moses hid his face, for he was about to learn the name of his God. It was a name unknown to his fathers and his fathers' fathers.

And it was the most sacred name of all.

Jehovah.

Throughout their long history, Jews have regarded this as the most holy, most glorious name of names. It was a name that gripped them with fear and filled them with awe. So much so that they wouldn't even pronounce it. So much so that every time they encountered it as they translated or copied the Old Testament, they would stop, take off their clothes, take a complete bath, put on clean clothes, and then—taking up a pen that had never been used before—they would copy the name.

Jehovah.

speaks to God's being or essence. When we read the name Jehovah, or LORD in capital letters, in our Bible, we are reminded of One who is totally self-existent. This is the One who, as Jesus said, "has life in Himself" (John 5:26).

The humanists say, "Where is God? Who made God? How did God come into existence? All things have to have a cause. Therefore, God had to have a cause. God had to come into existence at some point in time."

Everything that came into being came from the self-existent God who simply spoke and brought the universe into existence.

Of all the names of God, Jehovah (or *Yahweh,* as some render it today) is the name most frequently used in the Old Testament.

The first of 6,823 usages occurs in Genesis 2:4, where Jehovah is compounded with Elohim.

The name of Jehovah is derived from the Hebrew root that means "to be, to become." Therefore, Jehovah

Yet the answer to this faithless charge can be found in His very name—Jehovah. He is the self-existent Creator who made the heavens and the earth. His name says, "I always have been, I always am, and I always will be." Everything that came into being came from the self-existent God who simply spoke and brought the universe into existence.

Back at the burning bush, Moses was wrestling with the implications of God's commission to return to Egypt and free his nation from captivity. After four decades of lonely isolation, the command seemed utterly overwhelming. Yet in the backwash of his own inadequacy, impotence, and fear, Moses was about to learn the limitless power of a single name—the personal name of God Himself.

Moses said to God, "Behold, I am going to the sons of Israel, and I shall say to them, 'The God of your fathers has sent me to you.' Now they may say to me, 'What is His name?' What shall I say to them?" And God said to Moses, "I AM WHO I AM"; and He said, "Thus you shall say to the sons of Israel, 'I AM has sent me to you.'" And God, furthermore, said to Moses, "Thus you shall say to the sons of Israel, 'The LORD [Jehovah], the God of your fathers, the God of Abraham, the God of Isaac, and the God of Jacob, has sent me to you.' This is My name forever, and this is My memorial-name to all generations." (Exodus 3:13-15)

God is saying here, "I am that I am. I am the self-existent One. I am everything and anything you will ever need. Moses, it doesn't matter who you are. It doesn't matter what you have or don't have. It doesn't matter where you've been, where you find yourself now, or where I send you in the future. Nothing else matters,

God is Jehovah...He is there!
He has always been there, and He always will be there.
He will not change. He will not leave.

Moses. If I am with you, you have everything you need! My name is Jehovah. I am that I am. I am everything and anything you will ever need."

He is the eternal I AM.

He is the Alpha and the Omega.

What if I lost my job? What if everyone else forsakes me?

The eternal I AM says, "'I will never desert you, nor will I ever forsake you,' so that we confidently say, 'The LORD [Jehovah] is my helper, I will not be afraid. What shall man do to me?'" (Hebrews 13:5-6).

He will be who He is, and He will do what He has said He will do.

He is the same yesterday, today, and forever.

All of life is contained in Him.

Why do we look elsewhere? Why don't we rest in His unchangeableness? He has never failed. He cannot! He is Jehovah, the self-existent, covenant-keeping God.

Perhaps you feel the cold grip of fear as you read these words. You might find yourself wondering, *What am I going to do if my husband dies? What would happen to me if my wife passed away? What if my health should fail? What's going to happen when the kids move away?*

Further on in the book of Exodus, God explains to Moses:

I am the LORD [Jehovah]; and I appeared to Abraham, Isaac, and Jacob, as God Almighty [El Shaddai], but by My name, LORD [Jehovah], I did not make Myself known to them. And I also established My covenant with them, to give them the land of Canaan, the land in which they sojourned. (Exodus 6:2-4)

God was saying to His servant, "I am the same One who appeared to Abraham, Isaac, and Jacob and made My covenant with them. Now I am revealing Myself as the One who keeps His covenants! I am about to deliver My people according to My own Word."

He is the eternal I AM. He is the Alpha and the Omega.

He is the same yesterday, today, and forever. 🌿

God reveals Himself to His covenant people as the unchanging God who remains faithful to His Word throughout many generations.

He will be who He is, and He will do what He has said He will do.

Now, Precious One, what do you need in your life? What do you and I long for, deep in our spirits, in this age of broken relationships and broken vows?

We long for someone who will always be there. We need someone who will never change.

When I taught at one of our Teen Boot Camps for highschoolers on "Lord Heal My Hurts," I was so amazed and grieved by how many of these teenagers came out of broken homes. We had wanted to do something special on Father's Day, because the camp was in

session over Father's Day. But we just couldn't do it. There were too many kids in the camp without dads.

One precious teenage girl I met at the camp was hurting so desperately. Her mother was in the process of a third divorce. This teenager was the product of her mother's first marriage, and her baby brother was born during the third.

As this girl began to drink in the Word and understand some of the truths about God's names, she opened up to me one night.

"My mother is running around and talking divorce again," she told me. "But I don't think I can handle a fourth father! I've finally just come to love the father I have, and now I've got to go to a *fourth* father?"

She went on, "My mother's talking about moving again—and where we'll be moving is back in the fast lane. She'll leave me with the baby, and she'll be out every night. I hardly ever see her now. I'll *never* see her then. We've moved and moved so many times I can't even keep count."

But during the course of that week at camp, this young lady came to learn that God is Jehovah, and that He is there! He has always been there, and He always will be there. He will not change. He will not leave. He will not move. His love will never grow cold. He will always be there to comfort. He is the self-existent One, and everything and anything that she ever needs will come from Him.

When you need assurance that God is there keeping His promises, never changing, even though you have wavered in your promises to Him, run to your Jehovah. Trust in His name. It's a name that cannot change, because *He* cannot change.

He is Jehovah—the same yesterday, today, and forever.

And He's as good as His name.

Jehovah…the most sacred name of all.

CHAPTER SEVEN

JEHOVAH-JIREH

The Lord Will Provide

And my God shall supply all your needs
according to His riches in glory in Christ Jesus.

PHILIPPIANS 4:19

*I*t was just a ram with its horns caught in the thicket.

But to Abraham it must have been the most beautiful sight in all the world.

The sound of the animal's desperate thrashing in the dry brush was the most lovely, heart-swelling music he had ever heard. God had provided for Abraham for many years, but never at a more significant moment than this.

What that ram meant was *life*. Life for his own precious son—the child of promise.

The old man must have looked at that ram through a haze of tears and then cast his eyes toward heaven. In the joy and relief and gratitude of that moment, Abraham gave the Lord a name.

Jehovah-jireh—The Lord Will Provide.

Scripture paints the backdrop for us in Genesis 22.

God had told Abraham to take his son, Isaac, to Moriah and offer him as a burnt offering on a mountain of God's choosing. The text tells us that "Abraham rose early in the morning and saddled his donkey" and set out for Moriah with his son. But it *doesn't* tell us what kind of night Abraham endured before the morning of the journey. Did he sleep at all that night? Did he plead with God out under the stars? Did he weep and tear his clothing? The Bible doesn't say. It says only that he got up early in the morning to do God's bidding.

Abraham simply obeyed—though his heart must

have been breaking. He knew that his El Elyon was sovereign. He knew that his Adonai deserved unquestioning obedience. And, deep in his heart, he must have known that his El Shaddai would be sufficient for every need.

Abraham, Isaac, and two servants walked for three days. When Abraham saw the mountain in the distance, he left the donkey behind in the charge of the two servants. Then the man and his young son walked the rest of the way together: Isaac carried the wood; Abraham carried the fire and the knife.

What was Abraham thinking as he walked along with his beloved son? Scripture gives us a hint in the following exchange:

And Isaac spoke to Abraham his father and said, "My father!" And he said, "Here I am, my son." And he said, "Behold, the fire and the wood, but where is the lamb for the burnt offering?" And Abraham said, "God will provide for Himself the lamb for the burnt offer-

ing, my son." So the two of them walked on together. (Genesis 22:7-8)

What was running through Abraham's heart in that last, lonely trek up the slopes of Moriah? *God will provide. God will provide. SOMEHOW, God will provide.*

The author of the book of Hebrews gives us this insight:

By faith Abraham, when he was tested, offered up Isaac; and he who had received the promises was offering up his only begotten son; it was he to whom it was said, "In Isaac your descendants shall be called." He considered that God is able to raise men even from the dead; from which he also received him back as a type. (Hebrews 11:17-19)

God would provide, Abraham reasoned. God would keep His covenant—even if He had to raise Isaac from the dead! With grim determination, Abraham built the required altar, arranged the wood, bound his son—the love and joy of his life—and laid him on the altar on top of the wood. Did the father and son say their good-byes? Did they look at each other through tear-filled eyes? The Bible doesn't say. The text says only that "Abraham stretched out his hand, and took the knife to slay his son" (verse 10).

That's when Jehovah-jireh intervened.

That's when Abraham learned beyond all doubt that "The Lord Will Provide."

> But the angel of the LORD called to him from heaven, and said, "Abraham, Abraham!" And he said, "Here I am." And he said, "Do not stretch out your hand against the lad, and do nothing to him; for now I know that you fear God, since you have not withheld your son, your only son, from Me." Then Abraham raised his eyes and looked, and behold, behind him a ram caught in the thicket by his horns; and Abraham went and took the ram, and offered him up for a burnt offering in the place of his son. And Abraham called the name of that place The LORD Will Provide, as it is said to this day, "In the mount of the LORD it will be provided." (Genesis 22:11-14)

What was so significant about Mount Moriah besides being the place where Abraham offered Isaac? Second Chronicles 3:1 tells us, "Then Solomon began to build the house of the LORD in Jerusalem on Mount Moriah, where the LORD had appeared to his father David, at the place that David had prepared, on the threshing floor of Ornan the Jebusite."

From then on at Mount Moriah every temple sacrifice for sin would echo Abraham's words: "The LORD Will Provide [Jehovah-jireh], as it is said to this day, 'In the mount of the LORD it will be provided'" (Genesis 22:14).

Every lamb, every goat, every ram, every sacrifice

would point to the one ultimate sacrifice, God's ultimate provision for sin.

Since it is impossible for the blood of bulls and goats to take away sins, God prepared a body for His Son (Hebrews 10:4-5). Then at the appointed time, on the day of the Passover, Jehovah took that Son, His only Son whom He loved, and led Him to Mount Calvary. There, He laid Him on the cross.

But this time there would be no voice from heaven to stop the hand of death.

world. What man could not provide, Jehovah-jireh did! As Abraham said, by faith, "God will provide for Himself the lamb for the burnt offering."

And He has.

You and I deserve death. You and I deserve to pay the ultimate price for our sins.

But God provided the substitute. His own precious Son.

Have you, Beloved, gone to Jehovah-jireh and obtained by faith the provision for your sins, for your

His provision is complete! From His Son to mundane needs of daily life, the Lord will be true to His name. The Lord Will Provide.

This time there would be no ram in the thicket to take His place.

This time there could be no substitute.

This time the knife would fall.

For this Lamb—the spotless Lamb of God—was the only provision of Jehovah-jireh for the sins of the

death? Die you must: "It is appointed unto men once to die" (Hebrews 9:27, KJV). But "he who believes in the Son has eternal life; but he who does not obey the Son shall not see life, but the wrath of God abides on him" (John 3:36).

What will it be? Life or death? Heaven or hell?

Salvation or the terrible wrath of a righteous God?

Was eternal life all that Jehovah provided? No. There is much we need on this side of heaven in order to be more than conquerors.

The word for provide, *jireh*, in the Old Testament is literally "to see." But how do Hebrew scholars get "provide" out of it?

Because He is God, when He sees, He *foresees*.

Our all-knowing, ever-present, eternal Father knows the end from the beginning and thus, in His omniscience, He provides. Therefore, when Abraham responded in Genesis 22:8, "God will provide for Himself the lamb for the burnt offering, my son," he was literally saying, "God will see for Himself the lamb." The word *see* denotes provision, for when "Abraham raised his eyes and looked…behold, behind him a ram caught in the thicket by his horns" (Genesis 22:13).

I don't want you to miss this precious truth. I want you to know all that it means to call upon your Jehovah-jireh, for He provides more than your salvation. Not only has Jehovah foreseen your need for eternal salvation, He also sees your day-by-day needs! There is nothing too small or insignificant to escape His attention.

That is why Jesus instructed:

And when you are praying, do not use meaningless repetition, as the Gentiles do, for they suppose that they will be heard for their many words. Therefore do not be like them; for your Father knows what you need, before you ask Him. (Matthew 6:7-8)

Yes, our Father, Jehovah-jireh, sees our needs and knows them, yet He instructs us to pray, "Give us this day our daily bread" (Matthew 6:11).

Our all-knowing, ever-present, eternal Father knows the end from the beginning and thus, in His omniscience, He provides.

Do you feel silly asking God for bread when you can get it yourself? Do you feel that it is unnecessary to come to the sovereign Ruler of the universe with the seeming trivia of your individual needs? Do you wonder why God would even bother with you anyway?

Emily didn't wonder. As she returned home from one of our teen conferences, she discovered that her father had left. He had abandoned her and her mother without any provision for their future. But there was enough in the home for them to survive. There came a day, however, when Emily's mother went into the bathroom and found that the last piece of toilet paper was gone—and there was no money to buy another roll.

It was more than the mother could take. She fell apart and said, "How low can I sink? I can't even provide toilet paper!"

But Emily had learned the name Jehovah-jireh that weekend at our teen conference. She told her mother, "One of the names of God is Jehovah-jireh, and that means God will provide everything we need. Mother, let's ask God for toilet paper." And so they prayed to Jehovah-jireh.

The next day they were driving down the highway, and on the side of the road was a big, multiroll package of toilet paper.

His provision is complete! From His Son to mundane needs of daily life, the Lord will be true to His name. The Lord Will Provide.

O Beloved, our God, our Jehovah-jireh, is bidding us to come. We are coming to the One who is *for* us. "He who did not spare His own Son, but delivered Him up for us all, how will He not also with Him freely give us all things?" (Romans 8:32).

He is a God who is for you, not against you. In any test, you can lay your Isaac on the altar. You can worship Jehovah-jireh in obedience and know that whatever you need, the Lord will provide it.

He is The Lord Who Provides, and you can know Him by name.

CHAPTER EIGHT

JEHOVAH-RAPHA

The Lord Who Heals

But we have this treasure in earthen vessels that the surpassing greatness

of the power may be of God and not from ourselves...

Therefore, we do not lose heart, but though our outer man is decaying,

yet our inner man is being renewed day by day.

2 CORINTHIANS 4:7,16

Is there no balm in Gilead?" the sorrowing prophet wept. "Is there no physician there? Why then has not the health of the daughter of my people been restored?" (Jeremiah 8:22).

Gilead was a city in Israel known for its healing ointment. It was an effective balm that had both medicinal and cosmetic properties. The soothing salve of Gilead brought both healing and beauty.

But Jeremiah knew that his nation needed more than a topical salve. Judah's wounds went all the way to the soul. She was critically ill because of her sin.

There was only One who could heal her people.

There was only One who could bring health and beauty back to a sin-sick nation.

But would they turn to Him?

Centuries before the dark days of Jeremiah's era, God's people learned that there is a Physician. One who could bring refreshment. One who could take the bitterness of life and make it sweet.

His name is *Jehovah-rapha*—The Lord Who Heals.

The longer Israel journeyed with God, the more familiar she became with His character and ways. The revelation was progressive. When her deliverance from Egypt came, she fully understood why He was called Jehovah. For it was Jehovah who heard her cry and remembered the covenant He had made with Abraham generations earlier (Genesis 15:13-21; Exodus 3:7-8; 6:2-4).

Through that deliverance they also saw Him as Jehovah-jireh, for once again, through sacrifice, God provided what they needed. It was the Passover lamb that bought their release from the angel of death and the slavery under Pharaoh.

But even though released from Egypt (a picture of the world), God's people still bore some of Egypt's ways. The stench of Egypt was unmistakably discernible when the winds of testing blew. They would soon complain about bitter water, but the truth is, the bitterness was in their own souls.

Even so, Israel was about to see her God in yet another light.

They were about to learn of Him by a new name.

Then Moses led Israel from the Red Sea, and they went out into the wilderness of Shur; and they went three days in the wilderness and found no water. And when they came to Marah, they could not drink the waters of Marah, for they were bitter; therefore it was named Marah. So the people grumbled at Moses, saying, "What shall we drink?" Then he cried out to the LORD, and the LORD showed him a tree; and he threw it into the waters, and the waters became sweet. There He made for them a statute and regulation, and there He tested them. And He said, "If you will give earnest heed to the voice of the LORD your God, and do what is right in His sight, and give ear to His commandments, and keep all His statutes, I will put none of the diseases on you which I have put on the Egyptians; for I, the LORD, am your healer [Jehovah-rapha]." (Exodus 15:22-26)

Jehovah-rapha heals...but *what* does He heal?

I will never forget the day I was saved.

The night before, I'd been at a party. The only thing I remember about that night was a man named Jim. He had looked me right in the eyes and said, "Why don't you quit telling God what you want and tell Him that Jesus Christ is all you need?"

His words irritated me. My reply was curt.

"Jesus Christ is *not* all I need. I need a husband, I need a…" and one by one I enumerated my needs, numbering them on my fingers. At number five I thought I'd proven my case. I turned on my heel and went home.

For some time I had realized my lifestyle was unacceptable to God. I knew that were I to stand before God, I would hear Him rightfully say, "Depart from Me." My sins were obvious, and even I could not excuse them. For the first time in my life, I had seen my poverty of spirit. Although I had tried, I could not quit sinning. I had made resolution after resolution, only to give in again and again.

Finally I concluded that there was no way I could *ever* be set free. I just wasn't strong enough to change. I knew I was sick—sick of soul. As a registered nurse I had participated in the healing of many bodies, but I didn't know of any doctor who could heal my soul.

And heal myself? Well, that was impossible. I had tried.

When the morning of July 16, 1963, dawned, I couldn't face going to work. I called the doctor's office where I worked and told them I was sick. I'd come in on Monday. I hung up the phone and got Tommy off to day camp. At loose ends, I decided I'd bake a cake.

Suddenly, in the middle of the kitchen, I looked at Mark, hungry for love, hanging on to my skirt, and said, "Mommy's got to be alone for a few minutes." With that I rushed upstairs to my bedroom and threw myself on the floor beside my bed.

"O God," I prayed, "I don't care what You do to me. I don't care if I never see another man as long as I live. I don't care if You paralyze me from the neck down. I don't care what You do to my two boys, *if You'll just give me peace!*"

There beside my bed I found that there is a balm in Gilead.

There is healing for a sick soul.

There is a Great Physician.

His name is Jehovah-rapha, although I would first come to know Him as the Lord Jesus Christ, the Prince of Peace.

On that day in my bedroom, He applied the Cross to the bitter waters of my life, and I was healed of sin's mortal wounds (Galatians 3:13-14; 1 Peter 2:24). I had turned to Jehovah-rapha, the Shepherd and Guardian of my soul (1 Peter 2:25).

Only one Physician can heal the ills of our souls. Why look elsewhere? Why run here and there? Why not trust in the name of our Lord and rely on God (Isaiah 50:10)?

According to Exodus 15:26, health, healing, and obedience go together. As you read, listen carefully to the Spirit of God:

> And He said, "If you will give earnest heed to the voice of the LORD your God, and do what is right in His sight, and give ear to His commandments, and keep all His statutes, I will put none of the diseases on you which I have put on the Egyptians; for I, the LORD, am your healer."

Like it or not, there is a direct correlation between sin and sickness. Not just sickness of body, but also of spirit and soul. Am I saying that *all* sickness is due to sin? Please hear me carefully, for I have to answer that in two ways. First, if man had not sinned, there *would be no sickness* in our world. So in that sense, all sickness *is* due to sin. We must never forget we live in a sin-sick nation and world. Our wounds are great!

However, I do not believe that all physical or emotional illness is a consequence of personal sin. It *can* be, but it is not necessarily so. Some illnesses have other causes. Some illnesses may even be for the glory of God! (See John 9:1-3.)

But here is the question we must deal with, Beloved. Where do people turn when they need healing? Isn't it usually to other people? And when people turn to you for help, how do *you* deal with them?

So often people come to us at Precept Ministries seeking our counsel. Many have already been counseled, but to no avail. Sometimes the counseling has been ineffective because the counselee simply would not walk in obedience to godly counsel.

Often, however, that is not the case. In many instances we find that the counselor has evidently failed to deal with the *spiritual* problem. He or she has not sought wisdom from Jehovah-rapha nor asked Him for His diagnosis. He has not probed to see if there is sin that needs to be dealt with. Frequently we find that the counselor has not opened the medicine of God's Word and applied it to the subject's wounds.

Not too long ago we dealt with a man trapped by homosexuality. Although he had cried out for deliverance, he was still approached and propositioned by other men. He had received what many would consider the best of counsel from knowledgeable theologians. And yet never once did any of those counselors discern the demonic powers at work in him. The young man's tears were

bitter. Was he to fight this battle for the rest of his days?

As we prayed for and counseled this young man, God showed us what the problem was. Quietly and simply we claimed what was ours because of Calvary and because of our completeness in Christ Jesus. Then we took our authority over the Enemy.

Our friend was healed. He has a new radiance about him—his masculinity shows! He writes, "God has used you to set me free from the awful bondage of a lifetime."

It is not shameful to admit your need of healing. Until you do, there really can be none.

Whether an illness is physical, emotional, or spiritual, a person should *first* seek healing from Jehovah-rapha. Do you remember the tragic story of King Asa? Although he was a godly man for much of his reign, he drifted from God in his later years.

Scripture tells us:

And in the thirty-ninth year of his reign Asa became diseased in his feet. His disease was severe, yet even in his disease he did not seek the LORD, but the physicians. (2 Chronicles 16:12)

There is nothing wrong with seeking out physicians. But we must first bow before our Jehovah-rapha. Oh, He may and often does use doctors and hospitals and medicines and counselors as His instruments of healing. Yet the instrument is powerless without the Great Physician's power!

Seek Him *first*. Ask Him to examine your heart before a physician ever examines your body.

Sin affects our spirits, and the spirit can cause sickness of our emotions and our bodies. David wrote, "I am full of anxiety because of my sin" (Psalm 38:18). No, personal sin may not always be the cause of the problem—or even a contributing factor. However, we should pray fervently with David: "Search me, O God, and know my heart; try me and know my anxious thoughts; and see if there be any hurtful [wicked] way in me, and lead me in the everlasting way" (Psalm 139:23-24).

It's wise to have God search our hearts.

If His Spirit puts His finger on sin in our lives, we must deal with it thoroughly. Not to do so can stay the healing hand of God—or even bring further illness. As Solomon noted, "He who conceals his transgressions will not prosper, but he who confesses and forsakes them will find compassion" (Proverbs 28:13).

God always meets us at the point of our obedience, and there He comes over to our side. In Psalm 103:3, the phrase "pardons all your iniquities" comes before "heals all your diseases."

Are you in distress? troubled? weary? groping your way through personal darkness? Run into the strong tower of His healing name.

Only He can take your bitterness and make it sweet.

Heal me, O LORD, and I will be healed;
Save me and I will be saved,
For Thou art my praise. (Jeremiah 17:14)

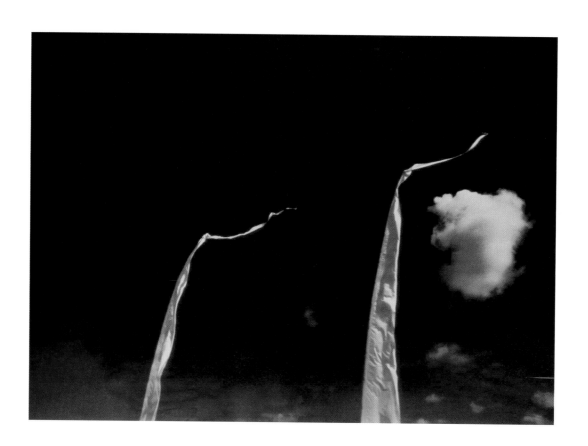

CHAPTER NINE

JEHOVAH·NISSI

The Lord My Banner

Thou hast given a banner to those who fear Thee,
That it may be displayed because of the truth. Selah.
That Thy beloved may be delivered,
Save with Thy right hand, and answer us!

PSALM 60:4-5

Are there days in your life when you feel utterly defeated? outnumbered, outflanked, and outgunned?

Do you ever feel overwhelmed and overcome by yearnings of the flesh that run counter to God's Word and His desire and plan for your life?

Where do you turn, Beloved? Where do you find the strength and will to stand fast and keep fighting the good fight? Where do you look for help when the Enemy comes in like a flood?

Turn to *Jehovah-nissi.*

Find your deliverance in The Lord My Banner.

Let your heart thrill at the victory that is ours in Him.

A banner in ancient times was an ensign or standard carried at the head of a military grouping. It showed the line of march or became the rallying point in a time of war. It didn't have to be a flag. Often it was a bare pole topped with a bright ornament that caught the light of the sun.

In times of battle, soldiers would look across the confusion and chaos of the battlefield for a glimpse of their king's banner. As long as the shining ensign was held high, they would fight with courage and confidence.

As children of God, the Lord Himself is our Banner. He is our confidence. He is the source of our strength in battle. We have only to look across the darkness and confusion of our life struggles to see our great King's standard lifted high. He is our shining assurance of victory.

That's the life-changing truth the infant nation of Israel needed to learn in the book of Exodus. They certainly didn't look much like a "nation" at this point in their history. They looked more like what they really were: a grumbling, distressed, disoriented multitude of former slaves.

But God's Wilderness University was in session, and the subject at hand was God Himself. His salvation. His power. His provision. His faithfulness. His victory. In verses 1-7 of Exodus chapter 17, Israel learned that the Lord could provide for the basic needs of life. The people had quarreled violently with Moses over the matter of drinking water. They even went so far as to accuse him of bringing them all out into the desert to kill them. The mood grew so ugly that Moses feared for his life. At God's instruction, however, Moses assembled all the elders before the rock at Horeb, and he struck the rock with his staff, unleashing a great gushing torrent of sweet, clear water.

Wonderful! But class was still in session!

Before the people had time to savor this mighty miracle of provision, a fierce enemy swept down out of the hills, bent on their destruction.

The Amalekites.

Then Amalek came and fought against Israel at Rephidim. So Moses said to Joshua, "Choose men for us, and go out, fight against Amalek. Tomorrow I will station myself on the top of the hill with the staff of God in my hand."
(Exodus 17:8-9)

You are not alone on the battlefield.

Look to the Lord your Banner! It is also His battle.

There was to be no white flag of surrender in this battle. No negotiations. No cease-fires. No peace conferences. God's instructions through Moses were very clear, "Fight against Amalek" (verse 9).

Before this day was over, Israel would learn a new name for their God. They would witness the power and deliverance of Jehovah-nissi.

And Joshua did as Moses told him, and fought against Amalek; and Moses, Aaron, and Hur went up to the top of the hill. So it came about when Moses held his hand up, that Israel prevailed, and when he let his hand down, Amalek prevailed. But Moses' hands were heavy. Then they took a stone and put it under him, and he sat on it; and Aaron and Hur supported his hands, one on one side and one on the other. Thus his hands were steady until the sun set. So Joshua overwhelmed Amalek and his people with the edge of the sword.

Then the LORD said to Moses, "Write this in a book as a memorial, and recite it to Joshua, that I will utterly blot out the memory of Amalek from under heaven." And Moses built an altar, and named it The LORD is My Banner; and he said, "The LORD has sworn; the LORD will have war against Amalek from generation to generation." (Exodus 17:10-16)

Moses' words were prophetic. He was saying, "This is not the only battle you're going to have with Amalek. Your sons and your sons' sons and on down through

The flesh will never stop attacking you and trying to drag you under. But...you have a Jehovah-nissi, and there is victory under that standard.

the generations are going to war against this relentless enemy. So you need to remember where to look for victory! The Lord is your Banner."

What is God telling us through this event? I believe He is showing us a great principle in the Old Testament for defeating *our* unyielding enemy, the flesh. I believe, as do other scholars, that Amalek is a "type" of the flesh. A *type* is simply an Old Testament foreshadowing of a New Testament truth. It's a picture from days gone by that helps you and me understand and deal with what faces us today.

Amalek was the first and constant enemy of Israel.

After the children of Israel had come out of Egypt through the Passover and crossed the Red Sea by the mighty salvation of the Lord (Exodus 14:13), and after they had eaten bread from heaven and had drunk water from the rock, the first enemy they had to deal with was Amalek.

Isn't the flesh your first and constant enemy also? The Christian life is a warfare, and it will be a warfare until you enter heaven. The flesh will never stop attacking you and trying to drag you under. But you need to remember that you have a Jehovah-nissi, and there is victory under that standard, that ensign, that pole of His name.

Later, Moses would write:

Remember what Amalek did to you along the way when you came out from Egypt, how he met you along the way and attacked among you all the stragglers at your rear when you were faint and weary; and he did not fear God. (Deuteronomy 25:17-18)

Note the phrase, "he did not fear God." The word *fear* means "to reverence, to respect, to honor God as God." Amalek had no respect for His great name.

O Beloved, can you see the parallels to our flesh?

The flesh cannot wait; its cravings must be satisfied now. Not later, but *now*! Like Amalek, the flesh knows no respect or reverence for God or for the things of God; rather, the deeds of the flesh are "immorality, impurity, sensuality, idolatry, sorcery, enmities, strife, jealousy, outbursts of anger, disputes, dissensions, factions, envying, drunkenness, carousing" (Galatians 5:19-21).

What is the greatest enemy of the child of God?

What is the first enemy a Christian has to deal with after he is saved?

What is it that stalks and attacks you from behind when you are weary?

Is it not your flesh?

A perpetual warfare is being waged in our bodies: "For the flesh sets its desire against the Spirit, and the Spirit against the flesh; for these are in opposition to one another, so that you may not do the things that you please" (Galatians 5:17). We can't do the things we please; rather, we must constantly be on the alert, ever cognizant of the promise that if we walk by the Spirit, we "will not carry out the desire of the flesh" (Galatians 5:16).

The flesh must constantly be put to death.

It can't be tolerated.

It can't be catered to.

It can't be spared in any way.

If it is, it will devastate you. Paul said in Galatians 5:24, "Now those who belong to Christ Jesus have crucified the flesh with its passions and desires." "Death to the flesh" is to be the battle cry of every child of God.

"But how?" you ask. And "Why?"

Because if you do not declare the flesh, with its passions and lusts, dead, it can kill you.

When will we agree with God and say, "For I know that nothing good dwells in me, that is, in my flesh" (Romans 7:18)?

When will we determine that we will walk by the Spirit who dwells within every believer?

When will we acknowledge that there is a war to be fought?

When will we rally at the standard of Jehovah-nissi and see the tide of battle turn?

True, the battle rages between flesh and Spirit as it

did between Joshua and Amalek in the valley of Rephidim.

Yet…*look up.* There on the holy mount of heavenly Zion is the Son of God with arms extended high, ever living to make intercession for you (Hebrews 7:25). All power and authority have been given to Him, and what is His is yours. You are a joint heir with Christ (Romans 8:17). Therefore, you have no reason or excuse for waving the flag of surrender. Stand firm. "Be strong in the Lord, and in the strength of His might" (Ephesians 6:10). Fight the good fight (2 Timothy 4:7). Of course there is a battle, "but thanks be to God, who always leads us in His triumph in Christ" (2 Corinthians 2:14).

You are not alone on the battlefield.

Look to the Lord your Banner!

It is also *His* battle. Note the words, "The LORD will have war against Amalek from generation to generation" (Exodus 17:16). It is the Lord's battle; victory depends on His rod being lifted up. The flesh is in opposition to the Spirit—God's resident, indwelling Holy Spirit.

What part do you play in it all?

Are you to sit in the grandstands eating hot dogs, drinking sodas, and giving a hoot and a holler every now and then? That is where most Christians are, and that is why our "team" is losing.

But you, O Valiant Warrior, are to put on the full armor of God and get on the battlefront. Under His banner, the victory is always assured, but apart from it, defeat is a certainty. When the banner of God's rod was not held high, Amalek prevailed. You can't do battle against the flesh under your own power.

O Beloved, if you don't learn anything else, learn this: Apart from Him you can do nothing (John 15:5). Only by abiding under the power, the standard, the banner, the ensign of your Jehovah-nissi can you have victory over the flesh, the world, and the devil, your enemies and God's.

What do you need to put to death in your life, child of God? Go to war and know that Christ is there with you, interceding on heavenly Zion's holy mount.

Victory is assured under the bright banner of His name.

CHAPTER TEN

JEHOVAH-MEKODDISHKEM

The Lord Who Sanctifies You

I bore you on eagles' wings, and brought you to Myself.

EXODUS 19:4

*D*o you have any friends who are so close, who are so loved, that just seeing or hearing their names encourages you?

🌿 You go to the mailbox, sort through the junk mail and bills, and then you see that familiar handwriting…and you're encouraged! You can't wait to open that letter.

🌿 You mechanically pick up the phone on a stressed-out day, mutter a quick "hello," and then you hear that familiar greeting on the other end of the line…and you feel encouraged before another word is spoken. You feel yourself start to relax. A smile finds its way onto your tired face.

🌿 You're in a conversation and someone happens to mention the name of your friend. That well-loved face appears in your mind's eye for a moment, and you feel a little surge of affection. Somehow, the day around you seems a little brighter—or the night a little less dark.

The names of our God can be like that to us—and so much more.

Once you know what they mean, once you understand what's behind them, just hearing those names can bring strength to your heart, a lift to your shoulders, and a spring to your step. Sometimes you'll want to say a name out loud. Sometimes you'll want to fall on your knees in worship.

El Elyon.

El Shaddai.

Jehovah-jireh.

Jesus…Emmanuel who is God with us, our Wonderful Counselor.

There's another name that's not as familiar to most of us. It's not even very easy to pronounce. And yet its meaning ought to bring a smile of relief and joy into your life whenever you hear it.

Jehovah-mekoddishkem.

That's the hard part. The meaning is the sweet part: *The Lord Who Sanctifies.*

After the Israelites set out from Rephidim,

They came to the wilderness of Sinai, and camped in the wilderness; and there Israel camped in front of the mountain. And Moses went up to God, and the LORD called to him from the mountain, saying, "Thus you shall say to the house of Jacob and tell the sons of Israel:

'You yourselves have seen what I did to the Egyptians, and how I bore you on eagles' wings, and brought you to Myself. Now then, if you will indeed obey My voice and keep My covenant, then you shall be My own possession among all the peoples, for all the earth is Mine; and you shall be to Me a kingdom of priests and a holy nation.' " (Exodus 19:2-6)

In other words, God is saying, "I saved you, Israel, by My mighty hand. I redeemed you, and now you are a set-apart people. You belong to Me!" The commandments He gave them on Mount Sinai would set them apart from all the peoples of the world as a unique people for God's own possession.

And the LORD spoke to Moses, saying, "But as for you, speak to the sons of Israel, saying, 'You shall surely observe My sabbaths; for this is a sign between Me and you throughout your generations, that you may know that I am [Jehovah-mekoddishkem] the LORD who sanctifies you.… For six days work may be done, but on the seventh day there is a sabbath of complete rest, holy to the LORD; whoever does any work on the sabbath day shall surely be put to death. So the sons of Israel shall observe the sabbath, to celebrate the sabbath throughout their generations as a perpetual covenant.' It is a sign between Me and the sons of Israel forever; for in six days the LORD made heaven and earth, but on the seventh day He ceased from labor, and was refreshed." (Exodus 31:12-13,15-17)

For the first time in the Word of God, the Sabbath is commanded and explained. This special day is to be a sign between God and Israel throughout all their generations. The purpose of the Sabbath was "that you may know that I am the LORD who sanctifies you" (Exodus 31:13) or "that you may know that I am Jehovah-mekoddishkem."

God is saying to them, "You are My people, and this is the way I want you to live. I want you to work six days, and on the seventh day I want you to rest. Why? Because I want to remind you—week in and week out, from now on—that I am the One who sanctifies you. You do not sanctify yourself."

What is so encouraging about that long name, Jehovah-mekoddishkem?

Just listen, Beloved.

It is the *Lord* who redeemed us, and it is the *Lord* who sanctifies us.

Who is the one doing the sanctification? Who is the one who makes us holy?

It's not you, it's not me, it's not a set of rules and laws, *it is the Lord*!

Now this word *sanctify* can also be translated *holy*. It means "set apart, consecrated, or separated unto God."

He gave them the Sabbath, and then He gave them His name. Sanctification would never come through the Law…it would only come through Him.

Now that's encouraging!

In 1 Peter 1:16, God says, "You shall be holy, for I am holy." And you say, "But, God, I have tried and tried! I've worked so hard to be holy, and I can't be! I'm so discouraged and defeated!"

The Lord says, "I am the Lord who makes you holy. Enter into My name. Enter into My rest."

And the Lord says back to you, "Hear Me, My child. I am *Jehovah-mekoddishkem.* I am the Lord who sanctifies you. I am the Lord who makes you holy. Enter into My name. Enter into My rest."

I believe that the Sabbath rest of the Old Testament is a picture of the eternal rest you and I are given after we receive the Lord Jesus Christ. That rest is a sign. God wants to show us something. He wants to show us, in His name, Jehovah-mekoddishkem, that salvation comes through resting in Him.

We cannot obtain salvation through our own efforts, no matter how honest and zealous and sincere those efforts may be. Salvation is of the Lord. By the same token, we cannot obtain holiness through our own efforts—no matter how hard we agonize and weep and labor. Listen, Beloved, you don't become holy by striving to be holy. You are *made* holy by God; therefore, you live a holy life *in response* to what He has already accomplished.

The Christian life is not what you do or don't do to make yourself holy. You do not sanctify yourself! It is only in Him that you find holiness and sanctification.

The constant observance of the Sabbath, week in and week out, was to remind the children of Israel that they were "a chosen race, a royal priesthood, a holy nation, a people for God's own possession" (1 Peter 2:9). As God sanctified Israel, so He sanctifies the church. And how does He sanctify us?

By the one perfect sacrifice of the Lord Jesus Christ (Hebrews 10:10-14).

By giving us the truth of His Word (John 17:15-19).

By calling us and enabling us to walk in purity (1 Thessalonians 4:3-8).

By providing us with His own precious promises (2 Peter 1:4).

Redemption wasn't the end of the Israelites' journey, it was the beginning. They had much to learn about worshiping and walking with a holy God. The Sabbath was their once-a-week reminder that it was the Lord Himself who made them holy.

Salvation isn't the end of our journey as believers either. It is the beginning! And just as we were powerless to obtain that salvation, so we are powerless to obtain holiness.

You will never make yourself holy by following a set of dos and don'ts. It is God who makes you holy and then gives you the desire to please Him. You live a changed life…not to gain heaven, but because you already *belong* to heaven.

The death of Christ provides for our redemption, for "without shedding of blood there is no forgiveness" of sins (Hebrews 9:22). The resurrection of Christ provides us with the ability to walk in newness of life through the gift of the Holy Spirit who sets us free from the law of sin and death (Romans 6:4; 8:2-4).

The God who sanctified Israel is the God who sanctifies the church.

The God who carried His people "on eagles' wings" is the God who carries you and me.

Call on His name and enter into His wonderful rest.

The God who carried His people "on eagles' wings" is the God who carries you and me.

CHAPTER ELEVEN

JEHOVAH-SHALOM

The Lord Is Peace

These things I have spoken to you, that in Me you may have peace.
In the world you have tribulation, but take courage;
I have overcome the world.

JOHN 16:33

*W*here do you turn when you're in distress?

Where do you run when you're troubled?

Where do you seek counsel when you're gripped with worry?

Not so very long ago, I found myself in a situation of deep distress. Torn with anxiety, I felt at times as if the pressure was going to push me right through the floor.

As the burden pressed in on me one morning, my first thought was to find my husband and just pour it all out to him. But Jack wasn't home that day.

Almost automatically I picked up the phone to call my colaborer—we're very close, and we talk and pray for each other all the time. I had my finger on the button to call. But something kept me from dialing.

I couldn't go to my husband. I couldn't go to Betsy. I couldn't go to anybody but the Lord. I had to have the mind of God on this matter.

Alone with God, I cried out to Him in my anguish. Like Hezekiah in the face of the besieging Assyrians, I got on my knees and just spread out my situation before the Lord.

And He heard my cry. Before I got up from that place of prayer, He laid the solution out before me. With no doubt at all, I knew what needed to be done. The fog of anxiety lifted from my heart. The path ahead seemed clear again. In place of distress, I felt peace.

As grateful as I am for my husband, my friends, and godly counselors, I was so glad that *this* time I had run right to the Lord. Instead of turning to the left or the right for refuge, I had hurried straight into the strong tower of His name. Like Gideon before me, I discovered firsthand that He is *Jehovah-shalom*—The Lord is Peace.

In some very dark hours of Israel's history, God revealed Himself to Gideon as Jehovah-shalom. He was the first to call on the Lord by that name. And by anyone's standards, this young man was a most unlikely candidate for divine revelation. Gideon's tribe, Manasseh, was one of the least tribes of Israel, and Gideon's family was the least in Manasseh.

Scripture says succinctly: "Israel was brought very low because of Midian" (Judges 6:6).

Why were they so low? It's not too difficult to guess the reason, is it?

Then the sons of Israel did what was evil in the sight of the LORD; and the LORD gave them into the hands of Midian seven years. And the power of Midian prevailed against Israel. Because of Midian the sons of Israel made for themselves the dens which were in the mountains and the caves and the strongholds. (Judges 6:1-2)

When the hour is dark, when the situation is desperate, when we are humbled and brought very low, we finally begin looking and longing for God's peace. Trembling, we grope through the darkness, longing for reassurance that all will be well.

When the angel of Jehovah appeared to Gideon,

True peace cannot be found in any other place than in a right relationship with God.

he was crouching in the dark confines of a winepress, threshing wheat in secret to protect it from the invaders. Now, I may not be an expert on ancient Near Eastern agriculture, but I do know one thing: You do not thresh wheat in a winepress. The idea behind threshing is to separate the heavier grain from the lighter chaff—and you need open air and a good breeze for that. But Israel was desperate, and you do desperate things when you're hungry and afraid.

> The angel of the LORD appeared to him and said to him, "The LORD is with you, O valiant warrior." Then Gideon said to him, "O my lord, if the LORD is with us, why then has all this happened to us?… The LORD has abandoned us and given us into the hand of Midian." And the LORD looked at him and said, "Go in this your strength and deliver Israel from the hand of Midian. Have I not sent you?" (Judges 6:12-14)

At first Gideon questioned this angel of the Lord and complained about his circumstances. How could God really love Israel, how could God really care about Gideon when they were all in such distress and danger and poverty?

Gideon did not yet know to Whom he was speaking. This angel spoke as Jehovah Himself, and when Gideon finally realized he'd been discussing politics and religion with *God*—face to face—he was rightfully terrified.

> He said, "Alas, O Lord GOD! For now I have seen the angel of the LORD face to face." And the LORD said to him, "Peace to you, do not fear; you shall not die." Then Gideon built an altar there to the LORD and named it The LORD is Peace. (Judges 6:22-24)

When do we first encounter the name Jehovah-shalom?

Where does God first reveal His name as The Lord is Peace?

In the presence of a man who was desperately afraid. In the presence of a man who was literally walled in by his circumstances. In the presence of a man who was worried and discouraged and had no peace in his heart.

But no matter what happened from this point on, Gideon could look back on an altar. He could look back at a moment in time when Jehovah-shalom said to him, "Peace to you, do not fear."

When the hour is dark, when the situation is desperate, when we are humbled and brought very low, we finally begin looking and longing for God's peace.

When Gideon's eyes were at last opened, when he saw that the Lord had taken a personal interest in his situation, when he realized that God was present with him in the midst of all this darkness and fear, he worshiped the Lord by a new name.

Jehovah-shalom. The Lord is Peace.

In the days to come, the Lord was going to put Gideon in some very unpeaceful situations. In some ways Gideon would be faced with more stresses and challenges than he had ever faced in his young life. Learning this business of being a "valiant warrior" wasn't going to be easy.

Beloved, do you ever feel as if you're trying to thresh wheat in a winepress? Do you ever feel surrounded by an enemy who presses in on you and tries to steal every grain of peace and gladness out of your life? Do you ever begin to wonder where your God is in the midst of your hurt and worry?

How rightly Gideon named that altar The Lord is Peace. True peace cannot be found in any other place than in a right relationship with God.

We cannot base our peace in the circumstances and situations of life.

We must not let our peace be centered in another

EMMAUS PUBLIC LIBRARY
11 EAST MAIN STREET
EMMAUS, PA 18049

man or woman—no matter how dear they are to us.

We dare not allow peace to depend on sunny skies and a full stomach and a balanced checkbook and a healthy body and a harmonious home. I believe that the Lord will sometimes allow situations in our lives that strip away the shallow, surface peace we have come to depend upon. He will allow us to be distressed and in turmoil, and we won't always be able to find the answers we need in our husbands or wives or friends or counselors.

In those times, as with Gideon, we need to discover that God is Jehovah-shalom.

As Paul wrote to the Ephesians, "He Himself is our peace." Once you really understand Him and worship Him as Jehovah-shalom, you can have peace, no matter what storms sweep over the horizon.

Jesus told His disciples that very thing in those last few hours before the Cross. These men were in terrible turmoil—and things were about to get much worse rather than better:

Peace I leave with you; My peace I give to you; not as the world gives, do I give to you. Let not your heart be troubled, nor let it be fearful....

These things I have spoken to you, that in Me you may have peace. In the world you have tribulation, but take courage; I have overcome the world. (John 14:27; 16:33)

Where do you run when you need peace?

Is your first response to go looking for a person or to pick up the phone?

Before you do, run into the shelter of His name. When you find Him, you find peace.

He *is* Peace.

Once you really understand Him and worship Him as Jehovah-shalom,
you can have peace, no matter what storms sweep over the horizon. ❧

CHAPTER TWELVE

JEHOVAH-SABAOTH

The Lord of Hosts

The LORD of Hosts has sworn saying,
"Surely, just as I have intended so it has happened,
and just as I have planned so it will stand."

ISAIAH 14:24

*T*here are times when you look around you and your first response is despair.

The odds against you seem overwhelming. The situation in which you find yourself seems unbearable. The forces arrayed against you seem overpowering.

You're overmatched, and you know it.

You're at the very end of your strength, and you feel it.

You're in deep trouble, and you sense defeat and darkness closing in on all sides.

O Beloved, there is a name you may call upon in times of conflict and warfare.

It is a name that makes the very pillars of the universe tremble.

Jehovah-sabaoth—The Lord of Hosts.

When there seemed to be no other recourse for deliverance, the children of Israel came to know God as Jehovah-sabaoth. It is God's name for man's extremity. And it is not until we, as God's redeemed people, find ourselves failing and powerless that we realize our need to run into the strong tower of His name.

The first two instances of this name in Scripture are in the opening chapter of 1 Samuel. It is in the final, decadent days of the judges, an era of great national stress and upheaval in Israel. In addition to the ever-present Philistines harassing and warring against her, the nation is about to endure a wrenching transition from theocracy to monarchy.

This is a time of darkness. A day of distress. An

hour of insecurity, change, and constant conflict. And it is in such a day as this that the name "the Lord of hosts" is first used.

> Now there was a certain man from Ramathaim-zophim from the hill country of Ephraim, and his name was Elkanah.... And he had two wives: the name of one was Hannah and the name of the other Peninnah; and Peninnah had children, but Hannah had no children. Now this man would go up from his city yearly to worship and to sacrifice to the LORD of hosts in Shiloh. (1 Samuel 1:1-3)

Because God had closed Hannah's womb, it brought her great distress from Peninnah, Elkanah's other wife.

> Her rival, however, would provoke her bitterly to irritate her, because the LORD had closed her womb. And it happened year after year, as often as she went up to the house of the LORD, she would provoke her, so she wept and would not eat....
>
> And she, greatly distressed, prayed to the LORD and wept bitterly. (1 Samuel 1:6-7,10)

Hannah found herself at the ragged end of endurance. Life seemed so bitter and unhappy that she didn't see how she could go on. Her food seemed tasteless, all the joy was drained from her life, and it seemed as if all she could do was weep. Scripture tells us she was "greatly distressed," "a woman oppressed in spirit." She seemed so out of control in her anguish that Eli the priest scolded her for being drunk in the sanctuary!

But what did Hannah do? Run away? Try to kill herself? Turn to the bottle? Surrender to some kind of numb apathy? What does a harassed, powerless woman do when she comes to the utter end of herself and finds life's conflicts unbearable?

She turns to the Lord of Hosts.

She calls on the name of Jehovah-sabaoth.

And she made a vow and said, "O LORD of
hosts, if Thou wilt indeed look on the afflic-
tion of Thy maidservant and remember me,
and not forget Thy maidservant, but wilt
give Thy maidservant a son, then I will give
him to the LORD all the days of his life,
and a razor shall never come on his head."
(1 Samuel 1:11)

This is a name for those who, in the midst of a
struggle, find their resources inadequate.

This is our name to run to when, from our perspective, there is no other help.

This name of God is a name that is yours to use in
the time of conflict and warfare. And listen, Precious
One, our warfare is going to get more and more open,
more and more blatant, as the day draws near for our
Lord's return, and the Enemy realizes his time is short.

This is a day to shelter in His name Jehovah-
sabaoth.

The name *sabaoth* means a "mass." In this case, it
refers to a mass of heavenly beings, a mass of angels, or
an army of heavenly hosts. Jehovah-sabaoth rules over
all the angelic hosts. He rules over all the armies of
heaven. He is Lord over all powers, principalities, and
rulers in high places.

It is the name David called upon as he stood all
alone against the Philistine giant in 1 Samuel 17. Now,

There is a name you may call upon in times of conflict and warfare.
It is a name that makes the very pillars of the universe tremble.

whatever you may have heard in Sunday school about the courage of this simple-hearted shepherd boy squaring off against Goliath, the stories just don't do this moment justice. Here was an untrained young man fresh from the sheepfolds. And he found himself standing virtually unarmed in the shadow of a nine-foot, battle-hardened warrior who was armed to the teeth.

Even King Saul, the man who ought to have stepped forward as the champion of his people, tried to dissuade David with some simple logic. "You are not able to go against this Philistine to fight with him," Saul reasoned, "for you are but a youth while he has been a warrior from his youth" (1 Samuel 17:33).

It was like the local Pop Warner junior-high football team going up against the Dallas Cowboys. It was like a fair-haired choirboy climbing into the ring with the heavyweight champion of the world. It seemed so ridiculous. Goliath evidently got a good laugh out of it too.

When the Philistine looked and saw David, he disdained him; for he was but a youth, and ruddy, with a handsome appearance. And the Philistine said to David, "Am I a dog, that you come to me with sticks?" And the Philistine cursed David by his gods. The Philistine also said to David, "Come to me, and I will give your flesh to the birds of the sky and the beasts of the field." (1 Samuel 17:42-44)

Listen to David's reply to this godless bombast:

You come to me with a sword, a spear, and a javelin, but I come to you in the name of the LORD of hosts, the God of the armies of Israel, whom you have taunted. This day the LORD will deliver you up into my hands…that all the earth may know that there is a God in Israel, and that all this assembly may know that the

LORD does not deliver by sword or by spear; for the battle is the LORD's and He will give you into our hands. (1 Samuel 17:45-47)

"You may be a mighty warrior with all your fearsome weapons and your big army behind you," David said, "but I come to you with something more powerful than sword or spear or javelin. I come to you in the

Jehovah-sabaoth rules over all the angelic hosts.

He rules over all the armies of heaven.... The battle is His.

name of Jehovah-sabaoth, God of the numberless armies of heaven. The battle is not *mine,* O enemy, it is HIS. It is not David the shepherd boy with whom you must contend, it is the Lord of Hosts!"

Have you learned that truth, Beloved? The battle is

His! He's the One who's in charge, and you can trust Him. He is Jehovah-sabaoth, Lord of Hosts; He is El Elyon, the sovereign, Most High God; He is Jehovah-nissi, your Banner of victory.

You do not face the enemy alone.

You need not fight your battles with weak weapons of the flesh.

The battle is His, and no one in heaven or earth—

angels or demons or Satan himself—can stand against Him.

No, His name is not some sort of talisman or magic cure-all. It isn't just repeating His name that brings deliverance. Scripture says clearly that it is the *righteous* who run into the strong tower of His name and find safety (Proverbs 18:10).

And for those who do run to Him, there is a refuge so strong and mighty it confounds the imagination. In this refuge "we will not fear, though the earth should change, and though the mountains slip into the heart of the sea; though its waters roar and foam" (Psalm 46:2-3).

Why is that, David? Why *shouldn't* we be afraid in the midst of such turmoil?

The LORD of hosts is with us;
The God of Jacob is our stronghold.
    (Psalm 46:7)

We can take David's word for that. And Goliath's, too, for "though he is dead, he still speaks."

CHAPTER THIRTEEN

JEHOVAH-RAAH

The Lord My Shepherd

Come, let us worship and bow down;
Let us kneel before the LORD our Maker.
For He is our God,
And we are the people of His pasture,
And the sheep of His hand.

PSALM 95:6-7

The problem with positive thinking is that there is often so little to be positive about.

We fail so often. Stumble so frequently. Lose our way so easily.

Positive thinking says, "Believe in *yourself*. You can do it. You can make it to the top. Tap into your human potential." Yet my experience tells me that sometimes I'm not very bright. Sometimes I'm not very strong. Sometimes I'm not very bold. Sometimes I can't seem to see any farther than the end of my nose. To be honest, sometimes I feel just like a *sheep*.

But that's not all bad, is it, Beloved?

It's not a bad life being a plain old sheep when I stop to consider that *the Lord is my shepherd*.

It is His very name. He is *Jehovah-raah*—The Lord My Shepherd.

As David captured it,

The LORD is my shepherd,
I shall not want. (Psalm 23:1)

Oh, what a marvelous revelation the Spirit of God gave us as He breathed these words through the pen of David! Clinging to the precious precepts of God is much better than dwelling on inspirational maxims or positive thinking, for He has magnified His Word above His name (Psalm 138:2).

Rather than believing in myself and trying to make

my own way through life, I turn to His precepts and, with faith in God, say, "I can do all things through Him who strengthens me" (Philippians 4:13). This is to think biblically, to believe what God says.

And what does God say about you and me?

He says we are like sheep.

He says it over and over again.

That's another thing God's Word says again and again. If we are weak, helpless sheep, then He is a loving, tender shepherd. He is Jehovah-raah.

Save Thy people, and bless Thine inheritance;
Be their shepherd also, and carry them forever.
(Psalm 28:9)

It's not a bad life being a plain old sheep when I stop to consider that the Lord is my shepherd.

"All of us like sheep have gone astray" (Isaiah 53:6); "My sheep hear My voice" (John 10:27); "We are…the sheep of His pasture" (Psalm 100:3); "I have gone astray like a lost sheep; seek Thy servant" (Psalm 119:176); "My people have become lost sheep" (Jeremiah 50:6).

All the positive maxims in the world can't change the fact that sheep are sheep.

What makes the difference in sheep is the shepherd.

He who scattered Israel will gather him,
And keep him as a shepherd keeps his flock.
(Jeremiah 31:10)

For thus says the Lord GOD, "Behold, I Myself will search for My sheep and seek them out. As a shepherd cares for his herd in the day when he is among his scattered sheep, so I will care for My sheep and will deliver them from all the places to which they were scattered on a cloudy and gloomy day.... I will feed My flock and I will lead them to rest.... I will seek the lost, bring back the scattered, bind up the broken, and strengthen the sick." (Ezekiel 34:11-12,15-16)

Sheep are the dumbest of animals. Sometimes I wonder if even chickens have it over sheep in the IQ department. Sheep are helpless, timid, and feeble. They require constant attention and meticulous care, have little means of self-defense, and easily fall prey to predators. If they do not have the constant care of a shepherd, they will go the wrong way, walk blindly into danger, eat the wrong food, and lap up the wrong water. If the shepherd doesn't lead them to new pastures, they will literally live out their lives in a rut. Sheep can also become cast down—stuck on their backs—and in that state, panic and die.

Do you see how shepherd-dependent these animals are?

And God says, "By the way...you are just like sheep."

Why did He create such dull-witted animals? I believe that in His sovereignty He had in mind a couple of important lessons for His people.

First, I believe He did it to show you and me our total, absolute poverty of spirit.

Second, I believe He wanted us to understand our desperate need of a shepherd.

He loves us so much! Remember when Jesus, tired in body as He was at the end of a long day, looked out

All the positive maxims in the world can't change the fact that sheep are sheep.
What makes the difference in sheep is the shepherd.

across the milling crowds that followed Him? Do you remember what Scripture says?

> And seeing the multitudes, He felt compassion
> for them, because they were distressed and
> downcast like sheep without a shepherd.
> (Matthew 9:36)

Praise be to God for His compassion! Praise be to Jehovah-raah who seeks out His sheep! Even though we do dumb things, even though we are not perfect, even though we all stumble in many ways (James 3:2), we can succeed and prosper because the Lord is our Shepherd. God designed us to be what we are so that we would see our need of Him. In Him, we find *all* that we need. Thus, we can say with total confidence and conviction, "The LORD is my shepherd, I shall not want" (Psalm 23:1).

The biblical picture of a shepherd with his sheep is filled with both tenderness and promise. The prophet Isaiah looked forward to the appearing of a Messiah who would come with great might and power and also with a wonderful kindness.

> Like a shepherd He will tend His flock,
> In His arm He will gather the lambs,
> And carry them in His bosom;
> He will gently lead the nursing ewes.
> (Isaiah 40:11)

Israelites reading these words would remember how a shepherd out in the wilderness would at times pick up a little lamb and tuck it into the fold of his garment. And as he walked along, that shepherd would talk to the lamb and caress it.

There would be times when a certain sheep in the flock would go astray again and again. Instead of learning to stay close to the security and provision of the shepherd, this sheep would foolishly wander off by itself and constantly get into trouble. How dumb are sheep? They will literally eat themselves right off a cliff. To get that last mouthful of grass, they'll plunge over the edge to injury or death.

In such a severe situation, the shepherd would be forced to break the leg of that sheep and then bind up the injury. Carrying the sheep in the fold of his garment, the shepherd would keep the animal close, carry it to pasture, and talk to it and sing to it until the leg finally healed. Then he would remove the splint and let him go. By that time, however, the sheep would have become so accustomed to the tenderness, warmth, and closeness of the shepherd that he wouldn't wander anymore. He would be content to stay at the shepherd's side.

Years ago, not long after we began our ministry, we were teaching some young people down in Mexico. One of the bright young men in the group was prone to wandering. He knew the Lord, but he would get distracted and tempted by this or that and walk away from the Lord. He was part of the group in the little chapel as I was teaching this material about shepherds and their care for the flock.

A couple of days later he hobbled into the room with a huge cast on his leg and a little grin on his face.

"Ernesto!" I said. "What has happened to you?"

"It was the shepherd, Señora," he said. "He broke my leg!"

The picture of the strong, patient shepherd leading his flock is woven throughout the Old Testament, from the book of Genesis on. As old Jacob lay on his deathbed, he spoke to Joseph about "the God who has been my shepherd all my life to this day" (Genesis 48:15).

But it isn't until we come to the New Testament that we see Jehovah-raah in all His fullness and amazing love.

Jesus said:

I am the good shepherd; the good shepherd lays down His life for the sheep.... I am the good shepherd; and I know My own, and My own know Me, even as the Father knows Me and I know the Father; and I lay down My life for the sheep. (John 10:11,14-15)

He is the Great Shepherd of the sheep. He is the One who came to seek and to save that which was lost. He is the Shepherd and Guardian of our souls. He is the Chief Shepherd who will return in glory with eternal rewards in His hands.

And how could the prophets have ever foreseen the wonder that He would not only be a shepherd, *He also would be a lamb*! The Lamb of God who takes away the sin of the world.

Revelation 7:17 says "the Lamb in the center of the throne shall be their shepherd, and shall guide them to springs of the water of life; and God shall wipe every tear from their eyes."

He is not only Jehovah-raah, He is Jehovah-jireh who provided Himself as the perfect offering for our sins and willful rebellion.

Have you wandered from His care and provision, Precious One? Seek Him, and you will find He is seeking you. Every single lamb matters to the Good Shepherd.

God designed us to be what we are so that we would see our need of Him.
In Him, we find all that we need.

CHAPTER FOURTEEN

JEHOVAH-TSIDKENU

The Lord Our Righteousness

Though I dwell in darkness, the LORD is a light for me....
He will bring me out to the light,
And I will see His righteousness.

MICAH 7:8-9

What do you do, where do you turn, when you have no hope?

No hope. Could there be a bleaker, more chilling phrase in the English language?

No hope.

Have you ever felt that way, Beloved? With hope extinguished like the smoking wick on a candle?

The nation of Judah came to that place in her history. She had refused to listen to God's words and had walked in the stubbornness of her heart. She had pursued and given herself to other gods (Jeremiah 13:10). The whole nation—except for a tiny remnant—had corrupted themselves.

The corruption was at the top, polluting even the priesthood. No longer could God accept them. He had to call their sins to account (Jeremiah 14:10). Judgment hung in the air. Nothing except repentance and a return to righteousness could stop it (Jeremiah 18:5-11). Yet when confronted with that option, the residents of Judah shook their heads and replied:

> "It's hopeless! For we are going to follow our own plans, and each of us will act according to the stubbornness of his evil heart." (Jeremiah 18:12)

It's too late for us, they were saying. We're too far gone. We've crossed the line. We're too addicted to evil. We're beyond hope.

Have you ever felt life was hopeless?

You had to agree with God. Your heart was deceitful and desperately wicked (Jeremiah 17:9). You knew it. Yet you were going to live the way you wanted to live. Nothing could change it. You were what you were.

Are there some hopeless cases? Helpless victims of their own sinful natures?

Is there no hope for hearts given over to sin and rebellion?

Yes, there is hope.

And it is in this dark hour of judgment and failure that God reveals to His people another of His names. It is a name of hope for those who have given up hope. It is a name of life for those who can see only death. It is a blazing, radiant beacon cutting through the darkness and pointing the way to heaven's gate.

Jehovah-tsidkenu—The Lord Our Righteousness.

The name was first revealed in a book of judgment—Jeremiah.

"Behold, the days are coming," declares the
   LORD,
"When I shall raise up for David a righteous
   Branch;
And He will reign as king and act wisely
And do justice and righteousness in the land.
In His days Judah will be saved,
And Israel will dwell securely;
And this is His name by which He will be
   called,
'The LORD our righteousness.'" (Jeremiah
   23:5-6)

It is a name of hope for those who have given up hope.
It is a name of life for those who can see only death.

If men and women are going to dwell with God, then they must be righteous. To be right with God, or to be righteous, means to be straight. It is more than goodness. It is to do what God says is right, to live according to His standards.

Yet Scripture is clear: We are *incapable* of attaining those standards!

> There is none righteous, not even one;
> There is none who understands,
> There is none who seeks for God….
> There is none who does good,
> There is not even one.…

> For all have sinned and fall short of the
> glory of God. (Romans 3:10-11,12,23)

Our hearts are so diseased with sin that we can't even begin to live lives that please God. So what can we do? What would it take? Bottom line, it would take a new heart.

A new heart? Impossible, right?

No. We can have a new heart.

> I will put My law within them, and on their heart I will write it.… For I will forgive their iniquity, and their sin I will remember no more. (Jeremiah 31:33-34)

> I will put the fear of Me in their hearts so that they will not turn away from Me. (Jeremiah 32:40)

> Moreover, I will give you a new heart and put a new spirit within you; and I will remove the heart of stone from your flesh and give you a heart of flesh. And I will put My Spirit within you and cause you to walk in My statutes, and

you will be careful to observe My ordinances.
(Ezekiel 36:26-27)

All this—a new covenant and a new heart—will come because of a righteous Branch named *Jehovah-tsidkenu,* the Lord Our Righteousness.

You can be right with God!

You can be *righteous.*

You need not live in an endless cycle of sin and failure.

You can have a new heart.

You need not turn away from Him (Jeremiah 32:40).

How? It is all wrapped up in understanding His name Jehovah-tsidkenu.

The righteous Branch in Jeremiah 23:5 is the fulfillment of God's promise to David that one of his descendants would rule forever. The righteous Branch who will reign as king and do justice and righteousness in the land is none other than God incarnate (God in the flesh), the Messiah, the Lord Jesus Christ.

The descendant of David by Mary would grow up "like a root out of parched ground" (Isaiah 53:2) and the Lord would cause "the iniquity of us all to fall on Him" (Isaiah 53:6). He was "pierced through for our transgressions…crushed for our iniquities; the chastening for our well-being fell upon Him, and by His scourging we are healed" of our sins (Isaiah 53:5; 1 Peter 2:24-25).

But would forgiveness of sins be enough? No!

Listen carefully to what Jesus said in the Sermon on the Mount.

For I say to you, that unless your righteousness surpasses that of the scribes and Pharisees, you shall not enter the kingdom of heaven.
(Matthew 5:20)

But how could that be when "all our righteous deeds are like a filthy garment"? (Isaiah 64:6).

How? Through the work of Jehovah-tsidkenu.

The Lord Our Righteousness.

At Calvary's Cross "He made Him who knew no sin to be sin on our behalf, that we might become the righteousness of God in Him" (2 Corinthians 5:21)—"even the righteousness of God through faith in Jesus Christ for all those who believe" (Romans 3:22).

There He hung, Jehovah-tsidkenu, made sin for you, so that you, by believing in Him, might be made His righteousness. What an exchange! Your sin—past, present, and future—for His own measureless, incalculable righteousness and purity. It's like taking a huge debt to the bank and coming home with "canceled" stamped over your debt—and a trillion dollars added to your account.

Yet we were not "redeemed with perishable things like silver or gold," but "with precious blood, as of a lamb unblemished and spotless, the blood of Christ" (1 Peter 1:18-19).

Can we be right with God? Only by receiving the Lord Jesus Christ.

But as many as received Him, to them He gave the right to become children of God, even to those who believe in His name. (John 1:12)

It is not too late. It is never too late while you still have breath in your body! Remember that as you pray for loved ones who seem so far from God—so set in their sinful ways. Jehovah-tsidkenu came to seek and save what was lost. His righteousness is near!

There was a day—a terrible day—when darkness came at noon, and the afternoon sun could not penetrate the gloom. It was a day when the earth rumbled and shook and men and women beat their breasts in despair. In the midst of the horror and darkness, a man in terrible agony, a man only hours from death, looked over at another man a few feet away.

If ever a man was beyond hope, this was the man.

If ever a man had reason to surrender to death and all the powers of hell, this was the man.

Yet…there was something about that man alongside him. Something that brought him a little surge of hope when there ought not to be any hope. In a voice choked with pain, the dying man turned and spoke to the one near him.

"Jesus…Jesus, remember me when You come in Your kingdom!"

And the One on the cross beside him looked over and spoke with certainty—and love.

"Truly I say to you, today you shall be with Me in Paradise" (Luke 23:42-43).

Run into the strong tower of His name, Beloved. The shining beauty of His very righteousness belongs to you.

What an exchange! Your sin—past, present, and future— for His own measureless, incalculable righteousness and purity.

CHAPTER FIFTEEN

JEHOVAH-SHAMMAH

The Lord Is There

Whom have I in heaven but Thee? And besides Thee,
I desire nothing on earth. My flesh and my heart may fail, But God is
the strength of my heart and my portion forever.

PSALM 73:25-26

What do you do when you feel alone… abandoned… forgotten by everyone—maybe even God?

What do you do when an iron bolt slides shut, imprisoning you in difficult circumstances? How do you keep your hope bubbling up like a spring? How do you keep your courage burning bright and strong?

In Babylonian captivity, the children of Israel faced seventy long years of exile (Jeremiah 29:10). With unbelieving ears, they heard the prophet Ezekiel describe how the glory of the Lord had departed from the temple back home in Jerusalem (Ezekiel 10:18-19; 11:22-24). How could this be? What would happen? What did it mean for their future?

They couldn't know it yet, but those hurting, displaced Israelites in Babylon were about to learn a new name for their God.

It would be one of the most precious names of all. *Jehovah-shammah.*

The Lord is There.

The name appears in the very last verse of Ezekiel. It refers to a future, earthly Jerusalem, the city that the Lord Jesus Christ will inhabit when He returns to earth to reign as King of kings and Lord of lords.

The city shall be 18,000 cubits round about;
and the name of the city from that day shall be,
"The Lord is there." (Ezekiel 48:35)

The word *shammah* is simply the word for *there.*

In biblical times a name usually described the character of the one who bore it. When God named this city Jehovah-shammah, He was assuring His people that He, Jehovah, would be there. Oh, what a message of encouragement this was to those in captivity! It assured them of a future and gave them hope.

We, too, need a future and a hope, don't we, Precious One?

Our world, for the most part, lives for today. "Give it to me *now*!" For many people, the future seems vague and uncertain, lacking in solid hope. Instead of looking out toward the horizon, they lose their vision and live only for their immediate happiness.

Scripture tells us, "Where there is no vision, the people perish" (Proverbs 29:18, KJV). No, they may not die outright...but something within them begins to wither away. Faith and hope begin to atrophy like muscles immobilized under a heavy cast.

This is essentially what happened to some of our American POWs during the Korean War. A number of these men never even tried to escape. This was unprecedented—especially in comparison to World War II. They resigned themselves to prison because they saw no future. They had lost their vision. They had let go of their hope. They shrugged their shoulders and simply gave in to their captivity.

This is also the story of many Christians! They have lost sight of that blessed hope, the wonderful prospect of being absent from the body and at home with the Lord, that glorious day when they will reign with Jesus on earth (Daniel 7:27). They have lost their will to fight because they have forgotten that their

Wherever you are, my friend, Jehovah is there.
He is waiting and longing to be your future and your hope.

"citizenship is in heaven" (Philippians 3:20). They can see and touch and taste and experience "now," but they can't fathom the glories yet to come. And they really don't want to even try.

Many Christians have become captives to the world and make no attempt to escape.

How can we keep from being worn down like this? How can we keep our vision clear and focused in a world that isn't our true home? How can we hold on to our hope?

By obeying God's Word, by meditating on its precepts, by clinging to it in faith…with all of our hearts.

> Make me walk in the path of Thy
>   commandments,
> For I delight in it.
> Incline my heart to Thy testimonies,
> And not to dishonest gain.
> Turn away my eyes from looking at vanity,
> And revive me in Thy ways…

> I opened my mouth wide and panted,
> For I longed for Thy commandments….
> Establish my footsteps in Thy word,
> And do not let any iniquity have dominion
>   over me. (Psalm 119:35-37,131,133)

And the more we open our hearts and lives to the ministry of God's Word and God's Spirit, the more we realize *He is there.* Wherever you are, my friend, Jehovah is there. He is waiting and longing to be your future and your hope. Do not be absorbed by your captivity, be absorbed with Him!

> Whom have I in heaven but Thee?
> And besides Thee, I desire nothing on earth.
> My flesh and my heart may fail,
> But God is the strength of my heart and my
>   portion forever. (Psalm 73:25-26)

It was difficult for God's people to believe He

would let Jerusalem fall. Yet they forgot another of God's names. It is a name I never hear mentioned anymore.

Qanna—Jealous.

In Exodus 34:14, God Himself said that His name is Jealous.

> Watch yourself that you make no covenant with the inhabitants of the land into which you are going, lest it become a snare in your midst. But rather, you are to tear down their altars and smash their sacred pillars and cut down their Asherim—for you shall not worship any other god, for the LORD, whose name is Jealous, is a jealous God—lest you make a covenant with the inhabitants of the land and they play the harlot with their gods. (Exodus 34:12-15)

There is a holy and godly jealousy, and God acted according to His name, just as He had warned His people He would.

In the face of their stubborn disobedience and rejection, His glory departed from Jerusalem. The cloud of His presence no longer rested over the Holy of Holies.

God had always been with Israel and Judah, manifesting His presence in one way or another. Yet it seems for the most part, they took His presence for granted. They just couldn't believe He would follow through and do what He said He would do. They couldn't believe He would depart and let Jerusalem, God's earthly Zion, be taken captive by the ungodly Babylonians.

Although God left Jerusalem, He had to come back, for He is Jehovah, a covenant-keeping God. Now you can understand how much it meant to God's people when God said, "The name of the city from that day shall be, 'The LORD is there'" (Ezekiel 48:35).

Jehovah would come in the person of His Son.

It wouldn't happen for generations, but the Lord was going to "return" to His temple. As Malachi, the last Old Testament prophet, foretold:

"Behold, I am going to send My messenger, and he will clear the way before Me. And the Lord, whom you seek, will suddenly come to His temple; and the messenger of the covenant, in whom you delight, behold, He is coming," says the LORD of hosts. (Malachi 3:1)

They would not hear another word from God for four hundred years following that prophecy. Yet Israel had His promise. The Messenger of the New Covenant would come to Jerusalem.

And come He did.

But most of Israel did not believe it was He.

In the beginning was the Word, and the Word was with God, and the Word was God.... And the Word became flesh, and dwelt among us, and we beheld His glory, glory as of the only begotten from the Father, full of grace and truth. (John 1:1,14)

Jesus, the "Mighty God, Eternal Father, Prince of Peace," came to Jerusalem. He entered her gates. He taught in her temple. He walked her narrow streets. He healed her sick and held her children and fed them on the shore and released them from demons. He ate with them and drank with them and wept with them and reasoned with them.

He offered Himself as Jehovah-shammah. He offered Himself as their true King.

But they would have none of Him.

When He approached, He saw the city and wept over it, saying, "If you had known in this day, even you, the things which make for peace! But now they have been hidden from your eyes.... You did not recognize the time of your visitation." (Luke 19:41-42,44)

And in the end, He suffered, bled, and died for them.

He came to His own, and those who were His own did not receive Him. But as many as received Him, to them He gave the right to become children of God, even to those who believe in His name. (John 1:11-12)

After His death and resurrection, Jesus went to be with the Father, but He did not leave us comfortless! Even now He is Jehovah-shammah to those who have believed on His name, for He dwells within us by His Holy Spirit. The Spirit of the living God lives within our bodies, like lovely, radiant treasure housed in a vessel of clay (2 Corinthians 4:7).

He was here as the Lord Jesus Christ. He is here now as the Holy Spirit. He will come again as the mighty King of kings to rule over the nations of this world.

How then are we to live? We are to live in the expectancy of "His Son from heaven, whom He raised from the dead, that is Jesus, who delivers us from the wrath to come" (1 Thessalonians 1:10).

God promised He would return to Jerusalem and that the name of Jerusalem would be Jehovah-shammah, the Lord is There. When He returns, then His Word through Ezekiel to His people will be fulfilled.

But, O Beloved, before all that or with all that, He must fulfill His Word to us, the church:

In My Father's house are many dwelling places; if it were not so, I would have told you; for I go to prepare a place for you. And if I go and prepare a place for you, I will come again, and receive you to Myself; that where I am, there you may be also. (John 14:2-3)

"And you will know that the LORD of hosts has sent Me to you." (Zechariah 2:11)

That is where I want to be.

Where He is. My Jehovah-shammah.

One day—on a day that will dawn but never fade—Jehovah-shammah will make His permanent dwelling among men. He will be as close to us and we will be as close to Him as His great heart has longed for since the beginning of beginnings.

And I saw a new heaven and a new earth;
for the first heaven and the first earth
passed away, and there is no longer any sea.
And I saw the holy city, new Jerusalem,
coming down out of heaven from God, made
ready as a bride adorned for her husband. And I
heard a loud voice from the throne, saying,
"Behold, the tabernacle of God is among men,
and He shall dwell among them, and they shall
be His people, and God Himself shall be
among them, and He shall wipe away every tear
from their eyes; and there shall no longer be
any death; there shall no longer be any
mourning, or crying, or pain; the first things
have passed away." And He who sits on the
throne said, "Behold, I am making all things
new." And He said, "Write, for these words are
faithful and true." (Revelation 21:1-5)

That day will come. But on this day, Beloved, rejoice in His nearness. Worship Him in the Holy Spirit. Feed on His Word. Delight in His people.

And rest in the strong tower of His name.

PHOTOGRAPHY